Practical NATS

From Beginner to Pro

Waldemar Quevedo

Apress®

Practical NATS

Waldemar Quevedo
San Francisco, California, USA

ISBN-13 (pbk): 978-1-4842-3569-0   ISBN-13 (electronic): 978-1-4842-3570-6
https://doi.org/10.1007/978-1-4842-3570-6

Library of Congress Control Number: 2018946546

Copyright © 2018 by Waldemar Quevedo

Managing Director, Apress Media LLC: Welmoed Spahr
Acquisitions Editor: Louise Corrigan
Development Editor: James Markham
Coordinating Editor: Nancy Chen

Cover designed by eStudioCalamar

Cover image designed by Freepik (www.freepik.com)

Distributed to the book trade worldwide by Springer Science+Business Media New York, 233 Spring Street, 6th Floor, New York, NY 10013. Phone 1-800-SPRINGER, fax (201) 348-4505, e-mail orders-ny@springer-sbm.com, or visit www.springeronline.com. Apress Media, LLC is a California LLC and the sole member (owner) is Springer Science + Business Media Finance Inc (SSBM Finance Inc). SSBM Finance Inc is a **Delaware** corporation.

For information on translations, please e-mail rights@apress.com, or visit http://www.apress.com/rights-permissions.

Apress titles may be purchased in bulk for academic, corporate, or promotional use. eBook versions and licenses are also available for most titles. For more information, reference our Print and eBook Bulk Sales web page at http://www.apress.com/bulk-sales.

Any source code or other supplementary material referenced by the author in this book is available to readers on GitHub via the book's product page, located at www.apress.com/9781484235690. For more detailed information, please visit http://www.apress.com/source-code.

Printed on acid-free paper

For Mariko & Karina

Table of Contents

About the Author xi

About the Technical Reviewer xiii

Acknowledgments xv

Foreword xvii

Chapter 1: Introduction to NATS 1

Using NATS for Messaging 2

Messaging Over the REST 4

Do Not Assume the Audience 5

NATS As an Always Available Dial Tone 8

Delivery Guarantees 10

Is NATS a Message Broker or a Message Queue? 11

A Brief History of NATS 12

Roots in Ruby 12

I Wanna Go Fast! 14

Cloud-Native NATS 16

Summary 18

Chapter 2: The NATS Protocol 19

Overview of the Protocol 19

Why Not a Binary Protocol Instead? 20

Setting Up the Environment 21

Connecting to NATS 22

PING and PONG 24

Sending and Receiving Messages 26

    Publishing Messages with PUB 26

    Registering Interest in a Subject with SUB...................................... 28

    Subject Names and Wildcards... 31

    Creating Queue Subscriptions for Load Balancing 34

    Limiting Interest in a Subject with UNSUB 36

    Publishing Requests 38

    Lowest Latency Response 40

Summary.. 41

Chapter 3: The NATS Clients 43

Features of a NATS Client 43

Using Connect.. 45

Customizing a Connection 47

Authorization Credentials.. 50

Using Publish and Subscribe 51

Using Publish 52

Using Subscribe 54

Using QueueSubscribe... 57

Removing a Subscription 58

Using Flush 62

Using Request 63

    The Classic Request/Response 65

    The New Style Request/Response... 67

A Note on Asynchronous I/O..67

States of a NATS Connection 73

Clients Reconnection Logic...77

Event Callbacks..80

Using Close 82

Summary...84

Chapter 4: Setting Up NATS 85

Server Configuration 85

Exposed Ports 88

Server Logging..94

    Logging Outputs 97

Configuring Authorization...98

    Extending the Authorization Deadline..100

TLS Options...101

Tuning the Defaults 102

    Increasing the Maximum Payload Size...102

    Extending the Deadline for Slow Consumers Handling 103

    Tuning the Keepalive Interval 104

    Tuning the Maximum Number of Connections 104

Server Reloading...105

    Reloading to Activate Tracing On-the-Fly 105

    Reducing the Number of Live Connections 107

Running NATS in Docker 108

Summary...109

Chapter 5: High Availability with NATS Clustering 111

The NATS Cluster Network Topology 111

Configuring a NATS Cluster from the CLI 114

Setting Up Clustering via the Configuration File 119

Explicitly Setting a Server Pool in the Client 121

    Disabling Random Reconnection Ordering 122

Bootstrapping a Cluster Using Autodiscovery 123

Monitoring a NATS Cluster State 124

On Autodiscovery and Load Balancers 126

    Setting Up a NATS Cluster Behind a Load Balancer 127

Summary 130

Chapter 6: Developing a Cloud-Native NATS Application 131

The NATS Rider Application 131

Scaffolding the Application 133

Defining a Base Component 137

    Customizing the Connection to NATS 139

    Enabling Components Discovery 141

The NATS Rider API 145

The Load Balanced Rider Manager 154

The Driver Agent 161

Summary 167

Chapter 7: Monitoring NATS 169

Server Instrumentation 169

    The /varz Endpoint 170

    The /connz Endpoint 175

    About /routez 187

About /subsz 192

Using nats-top for Monitoring 193

Summary...196

Chapter 8: Securing NATS..197

Connecting Securely to NATS...197

Configuring TLS in the Server...199

Securing the Monitoring Endpoint...200

Tuning the Authorization Timeout 201

Setting a Certificate Authority 201

Require Clients to Provide a Certificate...202

Setting Up a Secure NATS Environment from Scratch 202

Installing cfssl for Certs Creation 203

Defining the Security Roles 203

Creating a Custom Root CA 205

Securing the Connections from the Clients...206

Securing the Monitoring Endpoint...208

Securing the Routes from the Cluster 209

Caveats from NATS TLS Support..211

Not Possible to Use TLS Right Away 211

Limitations of Configuring TLS from the Command Line 212

Auto Discovery and Routes TLS..213

Summary...216

Chapter 9: Troubleshooting NATS 217

Types of Slow Consumer Errors 217

Troubleshooting Slow Consumer Protocol Errors...219

Subscriptions in Slow Consumer State...226

Routes as Slow Consumers in a NATS Cluster 228

Summary 231

Chapter 10: Advanced NATS Techniques 233

Using Inbox Subscriptions 233

Subscriptions with Heartbeats 246

Gathering Multiple Responses 253

Summary 256

Index 257

About the Author

 **Waldemar Quevedo** is a software engineer based in San Francisco and has been using NATS-based architectures for over five years. He is a core contributor to the NATS project and also maintainer of its Ruby and Python client libraries. In 2011, he became one of the early members of the PaaS team at Rakuten in Tokyo, which adopted Cloud Foundry and used NATS for its control plane. In 2015, he joined Apcera in San Francisco to work on a secure container orchestration platform, also built with NATS. In 2018, he joined Synadia to focus on the NATS project and its ecosystem. Waldemar has presented on NATS at a number of industry events, including StrangeLoop, GopherCon, and AllThingsOpen. He can be found on Twitter and Github as @wallyqs.

About the Technical Reviewer

Ivan Kozlovic was introduced to messaging when he joined TIBCO Software in 2001. He worked mainly on their JMS implementation, which Derek Collison created. In 2015, he joined Apcera to work on NATS. With his past experience, he was well suited to help maintain and improve it and was tasked to lead the NATS Streaming project. Since early 2018, he joined Synadia to continue his work and help grow the NATS ecosystem. With almost 17 years of experience in the Messaging space, he knows a thing or two about the challenges of building distributed systems.

Ivan holds a Bachelor's degree in Computer Science. He can be found on GitHub @kozlovic and on Twitter @ivankozlovic.

Acknowledgments

I would like to thank the whole NATS team who supported me in writing this book: Ivan Kozlovic, Colin Sullivan, Alberto Ricart, Ginger Collison, and of course Derek Collison, not only for creating NATS but also for his advice and mentorship through the years.

Special thanks to Brian Flannery for his outstanding work in the NATS community; Tyler Treat whose contents about NATS were a great reference and for his early advice in writing this book; Jaime Piña, Louis Woods, Peter Miron, David Karapetyan, and Oleg Shaldybin, who shared their advice and feedback on the contents; as well as everyone in the NATS community who has helped make it an exciting project to be a part of.

Also would like to give thanks to everyone in the Apress team who made this possible; Louise Corrigan whom I was fortunate to meet at AllThingsOpen and provided me with the opportunity to write the first book about NATS, as well as Nancy and James, who stepped me through the process and helped me revise the contents.

Finally, and most of all, I want to thank my wife Mariko for all of her support and for encouraging me to write this book.

Foreword

By some estimates there will be more than 75 billion devices by 2022 trying to be connected. That does not include the digital systems and services they will be trying to communicate with as well. These systems and devices will need a global, seamless, and secure technology to communicate. One that does not exist today—a global dial tone to connect everything. And once connected, this ecosystem will dwarf the global cellular network we know today and the Internet itself. I believe NATS will be that technology.

On October 30, 2010, the initial commit for NATS was made. NATS had been influenced through many years of designing, building, and using messaging systems throughout the 1990s while I was at TIBCO. In fact, I was designing a new system called Cloud Foundry that was to use a message backplane for discovery, events and command and control. Cloud Foundry was designed by a small team led by me at VMware. I had also pushed for the purchase of the company responsible for another popular open source messaging system at the time, RabbitMQ. The initial implementation for Cloud Foundry was using RabbitMQ, but was not meeting my overall goals. As most great projects start, so was NATS started, as something I built for myself and one that I could use to power the Cloud Foundry platform.

NATS was designed very differently from other messaging systems, even the ones I had authored in the past. It was very simple and performant, without any additional features, yet was always available and the basis for building extremely resilient platforms and systems. It could do request-reply, publish-subscribe, and load-balance between dynamic groups of queue subscribers. It also had a handy circuit breaker pattern to avoid overloading of client libraries making requests from an unknown large set of responders. A pattern I used often. It protected itself at all costs and strived to be always available, not letting any one client adversely affect the availability and performance for others. It works similar to the brain, in that all signals are fire and forget, or at most-once delivery.

In April of 2011 Cloud Foundry was launched and has since become one of the most popular platform technologies in the modern cloud era. Known for its scale and reliability, some due in my opinion to its original architecture and its use of NATS. Later in 2011 I travelled to Japan to speak to Rakuten engineers who had adopted Cloud Foundry. Among those engineers was an extremely bright and curious engineer, Waldemar Quevedo, or Wally for short. Wally constantly asked questions about Cloud Foundry and its design and gave me feedback, both positive and constructive, on ways it could be improved. As his curiosity grew, so did his interest in underlying technologies that powered the platform, technologies like NATS. Since that visit Wally has become an expert in NATS and its tooling, and is the author of several official clients, including Ruby and Python. He is a member of the core NATS team and has been working on NATS full-time for several years. He is a great speaker and educator and can be frequently seen at conferences. He is also a great friend.

In this book, Wally will walk us through NATS' basic concepts, the protocol and client libraries as well as the server. Along the way you will begin to understand not only the simplicity of NATS, but the power it can also provide in powering modern architectures and devices and driving toward a goal of connecting everything. If you want to become an expert in NATS, this book is a great place to start.

—Derek Collison, creator of NATS

CHAPTER 1

Introduction to NATS

NATS is a high-performance messaging system created by Derek Collison in 2010. It was originally built to serve as the message bus for Cloud Foundry, handling internal communication among components of the system. With the rise of microservices and cloud native paradigms, NATS has increased in popularity, becoming a mainstream piece of modern cloud architectures. The nats-io/gnatsd repository in GitHub now has over 3K stars and there is a growing ecosystem of tools and projects that us NATS as part of their architecture, as many have found it useful to address concerns such as:

- Service discovery

- Low latency communication

- Load balancing

- Notifications and events handling

In this chapter, you will learn:

- What NATS is and when to consider using messaging

- NATS' features and design

- A brief history of the project

© Waldemar Quevedo 2018
W. Quevedo, *Practical NATS*, https://doi.org/10.1007/978-1-4842-3570-6_1

Using NATS for Messaging

NATS is at its core a Publish/Subscribe (PubSub) system. The PubSub messaging model allows clients in a system to communicate without having to deal with the precise endpoints of where the services are located in the network, delegating this responsibility instead to the messaging system (see Figure 1-1). Clients become subscribers (or consumers) by registering interest into a subject, then whenever a publisher (or producer) client emits a message on that subject, the messaging system will deliver it to the available subscribers that were interested in that topic.

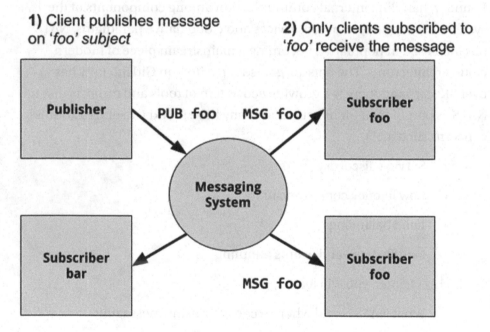

Figure 1-1. *Publish/subscribe messaging*

In NATS, this message delivery is brokered by the NATS Server (gnatsd). Clients establish a TCP connection to it and follow the NATS protocol, which was designed for simple and efficient PubSub messaging. Listing 1-1 provides a basic example of using telnet to interact with the NATS Server, using the demo.nats.io endpoint which publicly available for testing.

Listing 1-1. Hello World, NATS Style

```
telnet demo.nats.io 4222

INFO {"server_id":"EiRJABZmVpWQDpriVqbbtw",...,
"max_payload":1048576}
SUB greetings 1
+OK
PUB greetings 12
Hello World!
+OK
MSG greetings 1 12
Hello World!
```

The previous (albeit simple) example already shows quite a bit of the basic, yet powerful, feature set that NATS provides. We are making a subscription on the greetings subject (SUB), then publishing (PUB) and receiving a message (MSG) on that same subject. Here the message published is an opaque blob of data (in this case just an array of bytes with the Hello World! Characters, although we could have used any type of encoding as part of the payload). The NATS protocol is fairly straightforward with just a few number of commands, and this helps in making the implementation of the clients less complex.

Simplicity is a recurrent theme in NATS, as the project from its foundations had as a goal to be a lightweight messaging system and do less overall. Unlike other messaging systems, the NATS Server will only be keeping limited state for the client and only as as long as it has an established connection to the server. As soon as the client disconnects, the server will clear up any state related to the client, and it will not persist any messages and deliver them to the client in case it later reconnects, considering it a fresh new session with the server instead.

Another distinguishing factor of NATS is its *great performance*. NATS excels at enabling low-latency communication among services, and the way that the request response mechanism works in the clients was designed to address this specific use case in mind. Derek originally came up with the idea from a lesson learned during his time at Google, where making a request would involve a large number of machines responding back, but the client making the request would care only about a single response, namely the fastest one.

Thorough benchmarks done by Tyler Treat, who has spent significant time documenting the trade-offs taken by multiple messaging systems on his blog at `bravenewgeek.com`, demonstrate that NATS shows "predictable, tighter tail latencies"[1] in request/response round-trip benchmarks, especially when dealing with smaller messages. By default, the maximum payload size for a single NATS message is 1MB (although this can be tuned in the server).

Messaging Over the REST

Although these days HTTP-based REST APIs are very popular and best practices are well known, using messaging-based approaches instead for communicating offer a number of benefits when dealing with complex distributed systems. As previously mentioned, the PubSub model helps us decouple the services and instead just focus on communicating and sending the messages.

Consider for example what is involved in making an HTTP request. First, it is needed to look up an available endpoint (e.g., via DNS) of the service to which the client can connect and make the request. At this point it may still be possible that the endpoint is actually unhealthy, so it would

---

[1]*"Benchmarking Message Queue Latency"*
`https://bravenewgeek.com/benchmarking-message-queue-latency/`

be needed to retry and attempt to connect to another endpoint of the service. After successfully establishing a connection, the client will make the request and wait for the response back synchronously, then finally close the connection. In many programming languages, developers need to carefully manage the resources involved throughout. In Go, for example, it is a common programming error to leak sockets when using the *net/http* package, thus requiring careful code review or help via static analysis methods.

In comparison, a NATS-based request involves much less overhead, both in terms of the protocol and what is needed to keep in mind when making it. There is no need to have an established point-to-point connection against the service to which we are making the request; instead, the client ought to be connected to an available NATS Server already and just publish the message, then wait for the message containing the reply to be delivered asynchronously.

Do Not Assume the Audience

When using NATS, we are advised to never *assume the audience* of who is going to be consuming the message, as there can be multiple consumers for the same message for various independent reasons. NATS has support for wildcard subscriptions on a subject, and with enough permissions, it is possible to audit or trace every single message being sent through the wire without affecting how other parts of the systems are communicating. In Figure 1-2, there can be a number of "worker" clients subscribed to a subject that can reply to published requests, but all these requests are being logged by an "audit" client that does not reply.

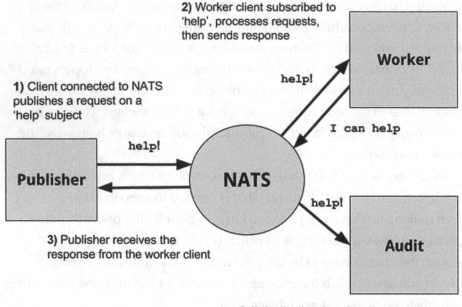

Figure 1-2. Example NATS request/response flow

NATS subscriptions by default have *fan-out* behavior and all the clients that have registered interested onto a subject will be receiving the message, but there is another type of subscriptions that make it possible to have a group of subscribers form a distributed queue with no server-side configuration so that messages sent are load balanced randomly to the multiple consumers (see Figure 1-3).

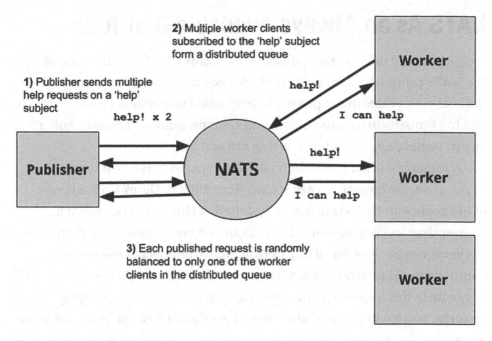

Figure 1-3. *Load balancing using NATS distributed queues*

It should be noted that the term *queue* is often misinterpreted by users new to NATS. That is, there is no *queuing* per se in the NATS Server. Instead, *queue* in NATS simply means that a message is randomly delivered to only one of the subscribers belonging to the same queue group (a name is specified when creating the queue subscription), unlike for regular subscriptions where a message is sent to all subscriptions subscribing to the same (or matching) subject. But for both pub/sub and queues, NATS subscriptions must be connected to a server in order to receive messages.

NATS As an Always Available Dial Tone

It could be said that the main design constraints that define the style of the NATS project are *simplicity*, *performance*, and *reliability*. Having these traits as core values of the project have resulted in a system that does much less in comparison to other messaging systems, notably it does not offer any persistence or buffering. It is true fire and forget.

A metaphor often used when talking about NATS is that it is intended to act as an *always available dial tone*. According to Derek Collison, one of his goals with NATS is to have a system that chooses to be available "rather than locking up around one client and one action to the detriment of everyone else; imagine if one person able to connect to the electric company could turn off the power for a whole city!". So NATS is the opposite in this regard in comparison to other enterprise messaging systems, and it will try instead to protect itself at all costs to be available for all users.

When using one of the available NATS client libraries, internally they will try to have an always established connection to one of the available NATS Servers, then in case a server fails, NATS will reconnect to another available server in the pool. NATS supports high-availability via a clustering mode that is set up as a full-mesh of the servers. As long as a client is connected to any of the server nodes in the cluster, it will be able to communicate with other clients (see Figure 1-4).

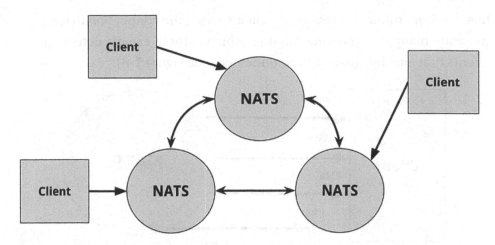

Figure 1-4. *Highly available NATS clustering full-mesh topology*

In case there is a connection that's accumulating too much data without draining it from the server, the NATS Server will protect itself and disconnect the client from the system, reporting a *slow consumer* error (see Figure 1-5). By default, if a client fails to drain the pending data that the server is holding for the client for over two seconds, the server will disconnect the client (this too can be tuned in the server). You can find more information on how to handle slow consumer conditions in Chapter 9, in the troubleshooting slow consumers section.

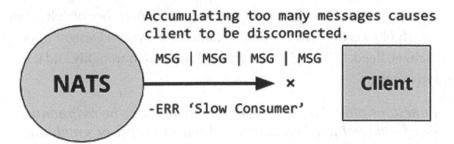

Figure 1-5. *Client disconnection with a slow consumer*

If a client does not follow the protocol properly, then it will also be disconnected. There is a PING/PONG interval happening that the client has to follow, otherwise the server will also reset the connection in case there are many PONG replies missing, which helps in eagerly detecting clients that may be broken or disconnected (see Figure 1-6).

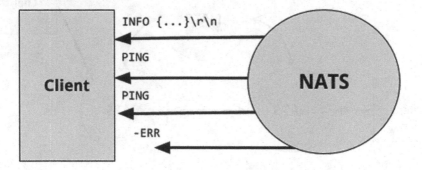

Figure 1-6. *Stale connection due to missing PONGs*

Delivery Guarantees

In TERMS of delivery guarantees, NATS provides *at-most-once* delivery, as a client has to be connected in order to receive the message. This may sound like a limitation, but it isn't really, as stronger guarantees can always be built on top. For instance, Request/Response in NATS is often used to ensure that a message has been delivered and processed by the intended recipient, offering an end-to-end delivery guarantee.

A recommended read for understanding the importance of delegating to the endpoints is the "End-to-End Arguments in System Design" paper from Saltzer, Reed, & Clark,[2] where this is discussed thoroughly and it is pointed out that:

> *Functions placed at low levels of a system may be redundant or of little value when compared with the cost of providing them at that low level.*

---

[2]"End-to-End Arguments in System Design" covered in *the Morning Paper* blog `https://blog.acolyer.org/2014/11/14/end-to-end-arguments-in-system-design/`

There is a cost in providing stronger type of guarantees, and for NATS to try to have those level of guarantees at its core would have meant less performance and reliability, thus actually limiting the type of applications that can be built with it. To address these concerns in separate, there is another popular project under the NATS umbrella named *NATS Streaming,* which acts as a layer on top of NATS providing *at-least-once* delivery type of guarantees. Under the hood, it is implemented using a Request/Response based protocol with the NATS client APIs and protocol buffers to add metadata to the message.

Is NATS a Message Broker or a Message Queue?

The definition of what a message broker is can be a bit fuzzy, as the terminology tends to be overloaded, thus making things confusing sometimes. Furthermore, the reputation of message brokers and message queues is often tainted due to the reliability concerns that arise as a result of supporting many features that NATS has been shying away from since the beginning of the project.

If a message broker is defined as a place where data is centrally stored and clients can connect at any time and consume this data, NATS clearly does not fit into that definition. Occasionally, newcomers to the NATS project ask for "queuing semantics" are told that it does not offer such type of usage.

For many of the classical notions of message broker or message queues, one can look at the NATS Streaming project instead, since those definitions would fit much better. Still, there is a middle ground in between where NATS-based messaging approaches can be more attractive and reliable, and covering that middle ground is one of goals of this book.

A Brief History of NATS

In 2017, the NATS project reached a significant milestone in that the v1.0 release of the project was made available by the team, as a way to represent that the NATS team considers its implementation to be battle-tested and stable enough already, with several production-level users running it for various years. NATS Servers are famous for their long uptimes and little maintenance and operational cost.

The road to get there has been quite interesting as well. In the first seven years, the NATS project has been through a a number events that have shaped the DNA of the project, and I'm briefly sharing these events in the following sections.

Roots in Ruby

NATS was originally developed for Cloud Foundry in 2010. The first implementation of the server was written in Ruby using EventMachine, same as many of the components from Cloud Foundry at that time. Listing 1-2 shows an example of using the Ruby client API.

Listing 1-2. Original Ruby Client API Example

```ruby
require 'nats/client'

NATS.start do

  # Simple Subscriber
  NATS.subscribe('foo') { |msg| puts "Msg received : '#{msg}'"
  }

  # Simple Publisher
  NATS.publish('foo.bar.baz', 'Hello World!')
```

```
# Unsubscribing
sid = NATS.subscribe('bar') { |msg| puts "Msg received :
'#{msg}'" }
NATS.unsubscribe(sid)

# Requests
NATS.request('help') { |response| puts "Got a response:
'#{response}'" }

# Replies
NATS.subscribe('help') { |msg, reply| NATS.publish(reply,
"I'll help!") }
```

end

Much of the foundations from NATS are present in this Ruby version of the server. We can recognize that the project had strong foundations: the protocol and the clients API are still pretty much the same to this day and there has always been strict backward compatibility among the versions of the server. This Ruby implementation was already stable enough and had decent performance as well. Available benchmarks at the time showed that one could get around 150K messages per second,[3] which was good enough for Cloud Foundry clusters, allowing it to support pretty big clusters with thousands of machines out of the gate.

Being originally an EventMachine-based system, asynchronous programming played a significant part of the NATS project from the start. The second official client was actually the Node.js client,[4] which naturally used async I/O as well, as it has to be done in Node.js (this client was also written by Derek since he was the main author of the project for a long time).

---

[3]"Dissecting Message Queues" by Tyler Treat https://bravenewgeek.com/dissecting-message-queues/
[4]Node.js NATS client: https://github.com/nats-io/node-nats

Though the Ruby-based server has since been deprecated (I removed it from being distributed along with the ruby-nats client in 2015), the original ruby-nats client gem is still being maintained by the team, and as of this writing it is still in use in some projects from Cloud Foundry maintained by Pivotal, such as BOSH.[5] Also, for many Ruby users, dependency of the client to EventMachine was often an issue, so now the team offers an alternative implementation in Ruby that does not depend on it.[6]

I Wanna Go Fast!

Derek Collison founded Apcera in 2012 to build a next generation container orchestration platform. There were many lessons learned from developing and operating Ruby, so he then rewrote the implementation of the server and a new client using the Go programming language. Apcera was one of the earliest adopters of Go (before it even reached 1.0) and made big bets on the language gaining popularity and eventually getting more adoption. Many in the Go community remember this. In fact, Rob Pike mentions Derek and Apcera in his 10-year retrospective[7] of the Go programming language.

Embracing the Go community even at those early stages paid off tremendously for the NATS project. Already in 2012 the Go-based

---

[5]Cloud Foundry BOSH: `https://github.com/cloudfoundry/bosh`
[6]Pure Ruby NATS client: `https://github.com/nats-io/pure-ruby-nats`
[7]"Go: Ten Years and Climbing": `https://commandcenter.blogspot.com/2017/09/go-ten-years-and-climbing.html`

implementation of the server was showing a lot of potential. This is from one of the first sharings from Derek on the new server version using Go 1.0.3[8]:

"We can process ~2M msgs/sec through the system, and the ingress and egress are fairly well balanced.

The basics of the architecture are intelligent buffering and IO calls, fast hashing algorithms and subject distributor/routing, and a zero-allocation hand-written protocol parser.

In addition, I used quite a bit of inlining to avoid function overhead, no use of defer, and little to no object allocation within the fast path".

Then at the first GopherCon in 2014, Derek shared[9] how he managed to improve the performance of the server even further to reach throughputs of around 6M messages per second at the time. Fast forward to 2017, after many more optimizations and releases of Go that keep getting better, that same benchmark now can reach around 18M[10] messages per second (see Listing 1-3).

Listing 1-3. NATS Go Client API Example

```
nc, _ := nats.Connect(nats.DefaultURL)

// Simple Publisher
nc.Publish("foo", []byte("Hello World"))
```

---

[8]NATS rewrite early benchmarks: **https://gist.github.com/ derekcollison/4227635**

[9]"High Performance Systems in Go" by Derek Collison https://www.youtube. com/watch?v=ylRKac5kSOk

[10]Benchmarks as of this writing: https://github.com/nats-io/gnatsd/commit/ b56ca22d1bfb571fa395a35fe698b0eb7f95e706

```go
// Simple Async Subscriber
nc.Subscribe("foo", func(m *nats.Msg) {
    fmt.Printf("Received a message: %s\n", string(m.Data))
})

// Unsubscribe
sub.Unsubscribe()

// Requests
msg, err := nc.Request("help", []byte("help me"), 10*time.
Millisecond)
```

Since the rewrite, Go plays an important role in the NATS project. The Go NATS client is now the canonical NATS network client implementation. There is a larger number of client implementations now, officially the NATS team supports C, C#, Ruby, Node.js, Elixir, Go, Python 2/3, Java, and Nginx.

Cloud-Native NATS

Microservices and cloud-native applications have also played a big part in the recent popularity of the NATS project. The NATS Docker[11] container now has millions of downloads in DockerHub and it was one of first official images to use the FROM scratch approach in order to provide a flat *binary only* container with few layers and no other dependencies. Also Prometheus is a popular tool for monitoring so the NATS team officially supports exporters[12] that can feed from the /varz monitoring endpoint from a NATS Server.

---

[11]Official NATS Docker Image: https://hub.docker.com/_/nats/

[12]Prometheus NATS Exporter: https://github.com/nats-io/
  prometheus-nats-exporter

Gossip-based auto discovery of NATS Servers in a cluster (shown in Figure 1-7) is an interesting feature that was added as a result of the feedback from the community. This was done in order to support certain types of deployments where it might not be known the network locations of all the nodes that will end up forming the cluster.

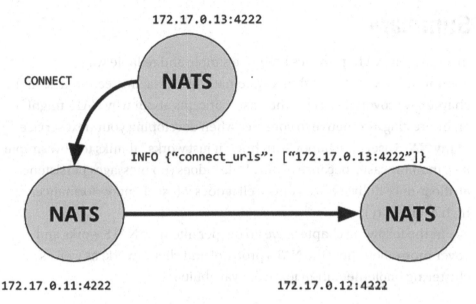

Figure 1-7. Gossip-based auto discovery in NATS clusters

Kubernetes is also an important part of the ecosystem so the NATS team also officially maintains an operator[13] for creating NATS clusters using the `CustomResourceDefinition`[14] feature from the platform.

---

[13]NATS Kubernetes Operator: `https://github.com/nats-io/nats-operator`

[14]Custom Resource Definitions: `https://kubernetes.io/docs/concepts/api-extension/custom-resources/`

Given how well it fits with the cloud-native paradigm and strong synergy with other projects in the ecosystem, in March 2018 NATS was accepted to be hosted as a project[15] by the Cloud Native Computing Foundation (CNCF).

Summary

In a nutshell, NATS provides us with a simple and reliable way to communicate very fast within a system using messaging techniques. In this chapter, we covered some of the basic concepts about why NATS might be an interesting alternative to consider when developing your next service. Many NATS users are happy with how "it just works," thanks to how simple it is, in many cases because of how little it does (no messages persistence, at-most-once delivery) and how well it does it (excellent performance, high availability).

In the following chapters, we go deeper into how NATS works and cover more about how the NATS protocol and clients work, as well as its clustering implementation for high availability.

---

[15]"CNCF to Host NATS": https://www.cncf.io/blog/2018/03/15/cncf-to-host-nats/

## CHAPTER 2

The NATS Protocol

NATS features a simple, plaintext-based protocol designed for fast and reliable PubSub messaging. Having such a simple protocol eases the task of implementing new clients, allowing you instead to focus on the fun parts, like improving the performance of the implementation.

In this chapter, we provide an overview of the protocol and take a look at each of the commands and their roles, as well as the different styles of communication that they enable together.

Overview of the Protocol

There are 10 commands in total that are used by both the client and the server. Each protocol line has to be delimited by the CRLF characters (\r\n). For simplicity purposes, I removed the characters from many of the examples. Table 2-1 provides the full list and a brief description of what each does.

Table 2-1. *The NATS Protocol*

Command	Sent By	Used To
INFO	Server	Announce metadata to clients
CONNECT	Client	Send credentials and metadata to server
PUB	Client	Send a message
SUB	Client	Register interest in subject
UNSUB	Client	Limit or remove interest in subject
MSG	Server	Deliver a message to client
+OK	Server	Ack client that command was processed
PING, PONG	Client & Server	Make a server roundtrip and keepalives
-ERR	Server	Announce errors

In the following sections, we take a look at each one of these commands and give examples of how they are used. One of the benefits of the protocol being in plaintext is that it also makes it easier to interact with the server manually, and in this chapter, we will be doing just that. Throughout this chapter we will be using a basic telnet-based session and sending raw bytes to the server showing the different PubSub features from NATS.

Why Not a Binary Protocol Instead?

Remember that the traits that the NATS project values are *simplicity*, *performance*, and *security*. The NATS team tries to keep a balance between them, and although having a binary protocol can possibly open the door to more performance, there is a trade-off in terms of maintenance and familiarity for developers, so a text protocol was chosen instead. Binary protocols in comparison are complex and hard to debug, which would have hindered the ability for community-led clients. Redis is another popular project that took a similar decision and has a large number of clients available for it.

Also consider that NATS is already pretty high performance with capacity to take throughputs of millions of messages per second and low latency, so a binary protocol wouldn't offer a big performance advantage.

Setting Up the Environment

First, you need to download one of the releases from the server available at https://github.com/nats-io/gnatsd/releases. There is a public endpoint at demo.nats.io that is also free to use (although keep in mind that it is insecure so others might be receiving the messages sent to it!).

Once you grab one of the release tarballs, you'll find the binary gnatsd, which is the high-performance version of the server written in Go. As of this writing, the latest release of the server is v1.1.0. For this chapter's purposes, any version is fine to use.

Next, let's start the NATS Server! Once it has successfully started, the server will bind to port 4222 (see Listing 2-1).

Listing 2-1. Starting the NATS Server

```
$ gnatsd
[58676] 2017/12/26 18:23:05.696873 [INF] Starting nats-server
version 1.1.0
[58676] 2017/12/26 18:23:05.697164 [INF] Listening for client
connections on 0.0.0.0:4222
[58676] 2017/12/26 18:23:05.697173 [INF] Server is ready
```

Connecting to NATS

Establishing a session to NATS can be done by simply using `telnet` and targeting the server (see Listing 2-2).

Listing 2-2. Using telnet to Connect to NATS

```
$ telnet 127.0.0.1 4222
INFO {"server_id":"65jPK8JboTBntebAiEHp5V",...,
"max_payload":1048576}
```

When the client establishes a connection to the server, the first thing that it will be receiving is an `INFO` message containing a JSON-encoded string with information about how to handle the connection to the server.

At this point, it is already possible to start sending messages. Let's try sending a small 5-byte `world` message on the `hello` subject, to which the server will reply with +OK (see Listing 2-3).

Listing 2-3. Publishing a Message to NATS

```
PUB hello 5
world
+OK
```

By default, the server handles the connections in *verbose* mode. This means that after each command, the server will reply with an +OK to indicate that it has processed the `PUB` command (see Figure 2-1).

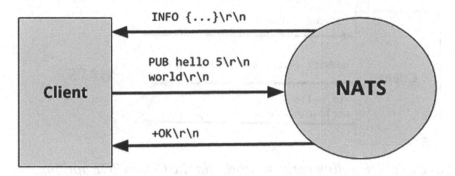

Figure 2-1. *Sending messages in verbose mode*

In hindsight, this +OK acknowledgement part of the protocol is not very useful. It does not tell us, for example, whether the message was delivered to a subscriber or provide any sort of end-to-end guarantee. Its only purpose is to signal that the server has processed the command. In this case, there are no other subscribers interested in the message, so no one will receive this message.

In actuality, all the available client libraries disable it by default. In order to do this, clients send a CONNECT command to the server with a payload encoded in JSON where it is signaled to the server that it wants to deactivate the *verbose* handling (see Listing 2-4).

Listing 2-4. Disabling Verbose Mode with CONNECT

```
CONNECT {"verbose": false}
```

Now if the client tries to publish the message again, the server will not reply with +OK anymore (see Figure 2-2).

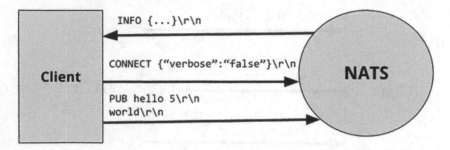

Figure 2-2. *Disabling verbose mode via the CONNECT options*

PING and PONG

Leaving an open connection to the server for around two minutes (this is tunable in the server via the `ping_interval` option), the client would have received from the server a PING message (see Listing 2-5), to which the client has to reply with a PONG (see Figure 2-3). If the client does not reply a couple of times, the server will disconnect the client (see Figure 2-4).

Listing 2-5. PING/PONG Protocol

```
$ telnet 127.0.0.1 4222
...
PING
PONG
```

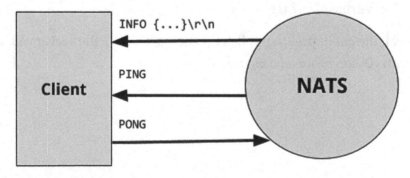

Figure 2-3. *NATS Server PING/PONG interval for keepalive*

Similarly, the client can also send PING messages to the server and the server will reply with a PONG. The client and the server connections must both rely on this PING/PONG interval in order to *autoprune* clients and servers and always try to keep a healthy connection. We cannot rely on TCP alone to tell whether the connection endpoint is gone.

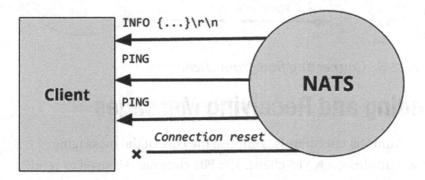

Figure 2-4. *Clients autopruning due to missing PONG replies*

The PING command also serves another important purpose. Since the NATS Server guarantees that all commands sent to the server will be processed in the order that they were sent by the client, a client can use a PONG reply as a way to determine whether the server has processed the commands that it has sent without issues. This provides a stronger guarantee than what we get from the +OK acknowledgement when using verbose mode.

This technique fits really well with the asynchronous programming model from the clients (for example, the awaited PONG reply can be modeled as a *future* pending to be resolved), and it becomes the basis of the implementation of the Flush API from the clients. This technique is also used during the CONNECTING stage of a NATS connection by the available clients (see Figure 2-5).

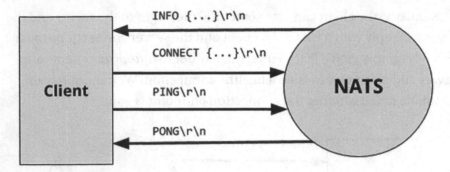

Figure 2-5. *Connecting flow from clients*

Sending and Receiving Messages

The PUB and SUB commands compose the core of the messaging functionality from a NATS client. The PUB command is used to send messages and the SUB command can be used to register interest in a topic. The server delivers messages to the client with the MSG command, and the client can also limit how many messages or whether to stop receiving them altogether via the UNSUB command. In the next sections, we go into detail about how each command works.

Publishing Messages with PUB

A client can publish messages by using the PUB command. Let's go back to the Hello World example at the beginning of the book in our telnet session to the server (see Listing 2-6).

Listing 2-6. Hello World Using PUB

```
$ telnet 127.0.0.1 4222
...
PUB greetings 12
Hello World!
```

In this example, greetings is the *subject* to which the client is publishing messages and 12 is the number of bytes representing the *payload size* of the message that is going to be sent to the server. Then after the line break, we can find the message itself, which in this case is Hello World! (see Figure 2-6).

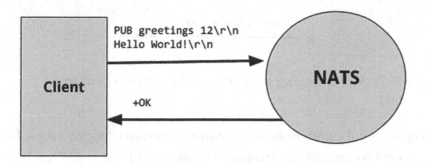

Figure 2-6. *Hello World using PUB*

The client should send *exactly* the same number of bytes as it has announced in the PUB control line; otherwise, the server will reset the connection, as it is not properly following the protocol. For example, if we add another exclamation mark and send instead 13 bytes but still announce 12 (see Listing 2-7), the server will send a parsing error response to the client and reset the connection (see Figure 2-7). The server is very rigorous in handling the protocol and does not hesitate to disconnect rogue clients.

Listing 2-7. The Wrong Number of Bytes Closes the Connection

```
PUB greetings 12
Hello World
-ERR 'Unknown Protocol Operation'
-ERR 'Parser Error'
Connection closed by foreign host.
```

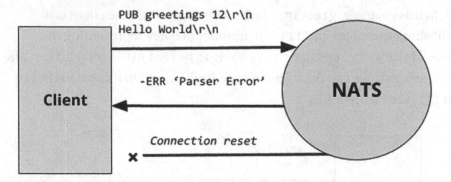

Figure 2-7. *Not following the protocol causes the client to disconnect*

The protocol commands are case-insensitive, so using lowercase for the protocol commands also works (see Listing 2-8).

Listing 2-8. Protocol Is Case-Insensitive

```
pub greetings 12
Hello World!
```

Registering Interest in a Subject with SUB

In order to receive messages, clients have to create subscriptions with the server by using the SUB command. Listing 2-9 shows an example of how to receive messages published on the greetings subject to a client.

Listing 2-9. Subscribing to 'greetings' subject

```
$ telnet 127.0.0.1 4222
...
SUB greetings 1
+OK
```

Here, greetings is the subject on which the client is registering interest and the number 1 is a *subscription identifier* that the client can use on the order to later match the messages delivered by the server. This subscription identifier will be particular to this subscription for the connection only and does not have to necessarily be a number either; a string identifier would have worked as well. Internally, the NATS clients use a counter, which increases by one for each SUB command sent to the server (see Figure 2-8).

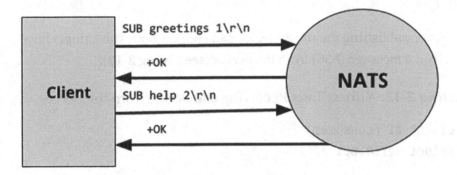

Figure 2-8. *Creating subscriptions with SUB*

Let's look at this in practice and open another telnet session that subscribes to greetings and another one for publishing (see Listing 2-10).

Listing 2-10. Pair of Subscribers on Greetings Subject

```
# Client #1 (consumer)
$ telnet 127.0.0.1 4222
...
SUB greetings 1
+OK

# Client #2 (consumer)
$ telnet 127.0.0.1 4222
...
SUB greetings any
+OK
```

Let's also add another one for publishing (see Listing 2-11).

Listing 2-11. Producer Client Sending a Hello Message

```
# Client #3 (producer)
$ telnet 127.0.0.1 4222
...
PUB greetings 5
Hello
```

After publishing the message, we can see that both subscribers have received a message (MSG) from the server (see Listing 2-12).

Listing 2-12. Subscribers Receiving a Message from the Server

```
# Client #1 (consumer)
$ telnet 127.0.0.1 4222
...
SUB greetings 1
+OK
MSG greetings 1 5
Hello

# Client #2 (consumer)
$ telnet 127.0.0.1 4222
...
SUB greetings any
+OK
MSG greetings any 5
Hello
```

The MSG protocol lines delivered by the server are followed by the payload that was sent by the publisher (see Figure 2-9). In the MSG protocol line, we can find the subject on which the message was published (greetings), the subscription identifier that matches the subscription done by the client (either 1 or any), and the byte size of the payload sent by the publisher (5 bytes).

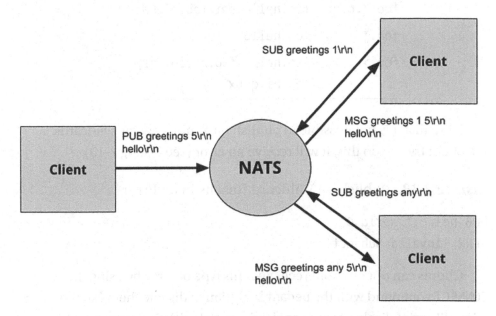

Figure 2-9. Example PubSub 1:N communication

Subject Names and Wildcards

The dot character (.) has special meaning as part of the subject. When using it as part of the subject, we can create namespaces that can be later matched via wildcards.

There are two types of wildcards available: the partial or token match wildcard (*) and the full wildcard (>). Table 2-2 lists a series of examples and matches using both types of wildcards.

Table 2-2. *Wildcard Support from NATS*

Subject	Matches
foo.*.quux	foo.hello.bar, foo.hi.bar
foo.*	foo.hello
foo.>	foo.hello, foo.hello.bar, foo.hi.quux

Note that it is not possible to publish on a subject using wildcards. If a client tries to do this, it will receive an error (see Listing 2-13).

Listing 2-13. Publish on Wildcard Results in an Error

```
PUB hello.*.world 0
-ERR 'Invalid Subject'
```

Clients can opt out from receiving this type of error by using the CONNECT command with the pedantic option to disable them (all the NATS client libraries disable pedantic checks by default). See Listing 2-14.

Listing 2-14. Disabling Pedantic Mode via CONNECT

```
CONNECT {"verbose":false,"pedantic":false}
```

The *full wildcard* in particular is very powerful, as we can use it on the top level and then inspect every message that is sent through NATS (see Listing 2-15). By adding a client that's using the full wildcard in the previous example, it would also get the message.

Listing 2-15. Using Full Wildcard to Receive All Messages

```
$ telnet 127.0.0.1 4222
...
SUB > 1
+OK
MSG greetings 1 5
hello
```

This is also very helpful for operations and helps debugging the messages that are being sent through NATS without impacting other parts of the system (other than a bit more load on the NATS Server). It is possible to limit the visibility of the clients by using the authorization features from the server (see Figure 2-10).

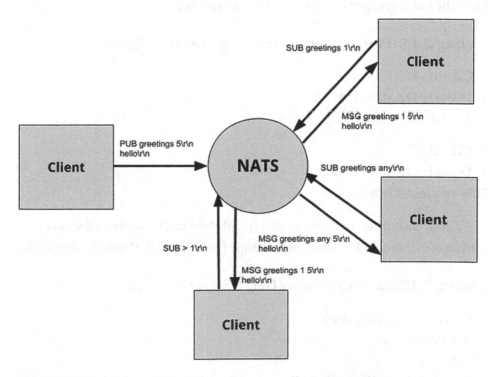

Figure 2-10. *Using full wildcard to tap all NATS traffic*

Creating Queue Subscriptions for Load Balancing

The type of subscriptions that we have seen so far make the server deliver a message to all the clients that registered interest in the subject (or a matching one). There is another type of subscription, called a *queue subscription,* which makes the server deliver the message to a single subscriber that's picked randomly from the same queue group, thus helping to decrease the network traffic and improve scalability.

Queue subscriptions are created by adding a *group name* after the subject when sending the SUB command (see Listing 2-16). In this example, two clients are making a subscription on the requests subject and joining a queue group named workers, using 5 for the subscription identifier of messages matching this subscription.

Listing 2-16. Pair of Clients Forming a Distributed Queue

```
# Client #1
$ telnet 127.0.0.1 4222
SUB requests workers 5

# Client #2
$ telnet 127.0.0.1 4222
SUB requests workers 5
```

Then, each time that a message is published on the requests subject, only one of them will receive the message (see Listing 2-17 and Figure 2-11).

Listing 2-17. Each Consumer Gets a Single Message

```
# Client #3 (producer)
PUB requests 5
first
PUB requests 6
second
```

```
# Client #1 (consumer)
MSG requests 5 5
first

# Client #2 (consumer)
MSG requests 55 6
second
```

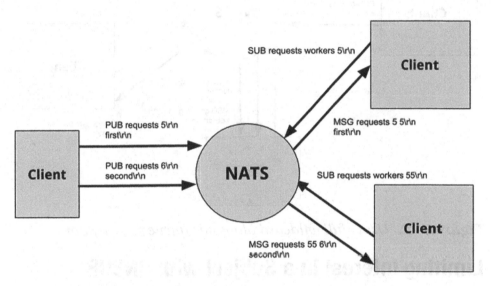

Figure 2-11. *Queue subscriptions random load balancing*

Note that multiple queue subscriptions and bare subscriptions can show interest in the same subject without them affecting each other. The NATS Server will deliver the message to each of them the same (see Figure 2-12).

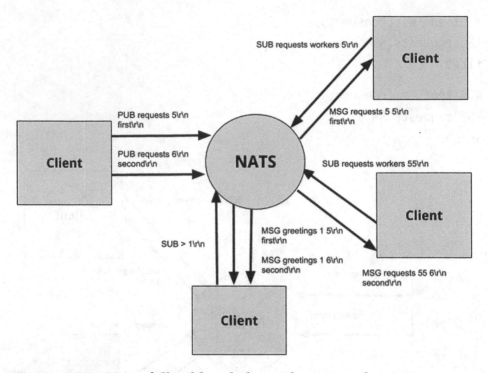

Figure 2-12. *Using full wildcard alongside queue subscriptions*

Limiting Interest in a Subject with UNSUB

After making a subscription to the server, a client sometimes may want to stop receiving messages related to the subject at some point. This can be done via the UNSUB command. The UNSUB command takes the *subscription identifier* (sid), which the client sent when making the subscription, and then optionally a number of max replies to receive before removing interest on the subject.

In Listing 2-18, the client is making a subscription on the requests subject, registering it with 5 as the sid, and then telling the server that it does not want to receive more than a single message.

Listing 2-18. Removing Interest in Subscription

```
SUB requests 5
+OK
UNSUB 5 1
+OK
```

Then, if another client publishes two messages on the `requests` subject (see Listing 2-19), only the first message will be delivered and the server will *auto unsubscribe* the client so it stops receiving messages on that subscription (see Figure 2-13).

Listing 2-19. Client Publishing Two Messages

```
# Client 2
PUB requests 4
help
+OK
PUB requests 5
help!
+OK

# Client 1
MSG requests 5 4
help
+OK
```

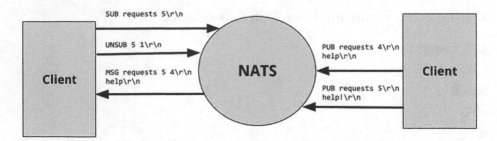

Figure 2-13. *Setting the max number of messages to receive on a subscription*

To remove interest in a subject instantly instead of after a number of replies, only the sid is needed (see Listing 2-20).

Listing 2-20. Removing Interest in a Subscription

```
SUB requests 5
+OK
UNSUB 5
+OK
```

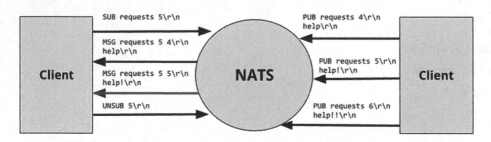

Figure 2-14. *Client does not receive last message after UNSUB*

Publishing Requests

This is where all of it comes together in order to support one-to-one Request/Response functionality. When sending a PUB command to the server, it is possible to also tag the message published with an optional reply subject (see Listing 2-21).

Listing 2-21. Publishing a Request with a Reply Subject

```
PUB help please 5
help!
```

Then, if there are other subscribers interested in the help subject, as shown in Listing 2-22, they will receive the message along with the reply subject.

Listing 2-22. Request/Response Example with PUB/SUB

```
# Client #1 is available for requests on subject
SUB requests 1

# Client #2 sends a request
SUB reply 90
PUB requests reply 5
help!

# Client #1 receives the request along with reply subject
MSG requests 1 reply 5
help!
```

The client that received the help! message is aware now of the reply subject, which has to be used (reply) in order to communicate directly with the client that sent the message and reply with a response (see Listing 2-23 and Figure 2-15).

Listing 2-23. Subscribers Receiving a Message from the Server

```
# Client #1 replies with response
SUB requests 1
MSG requests 1 reply 5
help!
PUB reply 11
I can help!
```

```
# Client #2 receives the response
SUB reply 90
PUB requests reply 5
help!
MSG reply 90 11
I can help!
```

Note that the inbox subscription itself is just a bare subscription and there is nothing special about it. The NATS clients then rely on making the subscription inboxes names unique enough that it would be extremely unlikely to have collisions in the unique identifier for the inbox. For this, the NATS Go client uses the NUID library to generate reply subjects of 22 bytes (more about the NATS client internals in the next chapter).

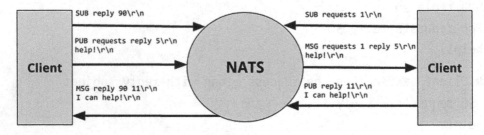

Figure 2-15. *PubSub-based Request/Response implementation*

Lowest Latency Response

If the subscription is not part of a *queue subscription group*, the first response that we get by definition is the response with the *lowest latency*, which is one of the key cases for which NATS is suited.

Clients can also take advantage of this property along with the UNSUB command to ensure that the server only the delivers the fastest response to the client (see Figure 2-16). This technique served as the original implementation of the Request/Response; there is a new style of making requests as well. Both styles covered in detail in next chapter.

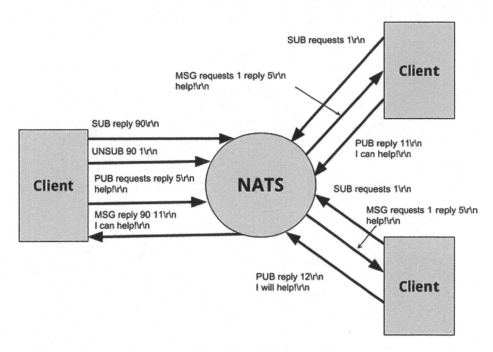

Figure 2-16. *Request/Response limiting to single fastest reply*

Summary

In this chapter, we got an overview of the protocol's commands and learned some of the techniques working under the hood of the NATS client library implementations. In the next chapter, we take a look at the client APIs and how they leverage the features from the protocol.

CHAPTER 3

The NATS Clients

As covered in the previous chapter, NATS uses a fairly simple protocol that
alleviates the task of implementing clients that can interact with the server.
Thanks to the protocol being very simple, many times it is also possible to
further focus on optimizing the clients to provide a highly performant and
efficient implementation.

The NATS clients have an easy-to-use API built on top of the NATS
protocol, and in this chapter, we take a look at their feature set and
expected behavior in detail. We do this in order to have a good foundation
for building NATS-based applications later in the book.

The examples in this chapter mostly use the Go NATS client, which
is now the reference implementation of a client for NATS, so some basic
familiarity with the Go language would be useful.

Features of a NATS Client

In the previous chapter, a basic `telnet` session was used to demonstrate
the feature set from the NATS Server by using the raw protocol commands.
Clients for NATS can be extremely simple if needed, as it takes very little to
follow the protocol. However, client language libraries require a bit more
behavior in order to make the implementation more reliable.

The NATS clients work asynchronously under the hood and many
times use efficient buffering and write coalescing techniques that improve
the publishing performance and consumption of messages. They also

© Waldemar Quevedo 2018
W. Quevedo, *Practical NATS*, https://doi.org/10.1007/978-1-4842-3570-6_3

have built-in reconnection logic support to failover to other available NATS Servers in case of a disconnection to the server has occurred, cluster autodiscovery re-configuration via server gossip updates (using the INFO protocol), and several types of event callbacks that are also triggered asynchronously during the reconnection process or when the server sends a protocol error to the client.

When connected, the NATS clients try to always keep a single, established TCP connection to a server. Just like the server, they also should implement their own PING/PONG interval in order to detect unhealthy connections and disconnect in case too many PONGs are missing from the server.

The API available in the clients has been evolving throughout the years and some of the earlier ones feature a slightly dissimilar API from the one available in the Go client. Still, all official NATS clients have at least the methods described in Table 3-1. These can be considered to be the core API from NATS.

Table 3-1. *The NATS Client API*

Command	Used To
Connect	Establishes a connection to a server
Close	Wraps up a connection to a server
Request	Sends a message expecting a response
Publish	Sends a message
Subscribe	Creates a subscription
Unsubscribe	Removes a subscription
Flush	Sends pending data and makes a server roundtrip

In the rest of this chapter, we look at how each of these methods works in detail, as well as describe the overall behavior from the client.

Using Connect

In order to connect to a server, clients have a Connect function where the location of a NATS Server can be specified, using either nats:// or tls:// as the scheme in the URL. In Listing 3-1, the client is connecting to the demo.nats.io endpoint using the default port 4222 from the server.

Listing 3-1. Connecting to a NATS Server

```go
package main

import (
        "log"
        "runtime"

        "github.com/nats-io/go-nats"
)

func main() {
        nc, err := nats.Connect("nats://demo.nats.io:4222")
        if err != nil {
                log.Fatalf("Error: %s", err)
        }
        nc.Subscribe("greeting", func(m *nats.Msg) {
                log.Printf("[Received] %s", string(m.Data))
        })
        nc.Publish("greeting", []byte("hello world"))
        runtime.Goexit()
}
```

To establish a secure connection, `tls://` as a scheme can be used instead. In Listing 3-2 a secure connection is set by using the configured secure port from the `demo.nats.io`.

Listing 3-2. Secure Connection to a NATS Server

```go
package main

import (
        "log"
        "runtime"

        "github.com/nats-io/go-nats"
)

func main() {
        nc, err := nats.Connect("tls://demo.nats.io:4443")
        if err != nil {
                log.Fatalf("Error: %s", err)
        }
        nc.Subscribe("greeting", func(m *nats.Msg) {
                log.Printf("[Received] %s", string(m.Data))
        })
        nc.Publish("greeting", []byte("hello world"))
        runtime.Goexit()
}
```

Internally, Connect uses the CONNECT command from the protocol after establishing a TCP connection to both announce client metadata to the server and handle the credentials. If there is a secure connection, it is after the connection has already been upgraded to TLS that the client will be sending the CONNECT command.

If the client fails to establish a connection on the first attempt, it will stop attempting to establish a connection in order to fail fast. Only after having established a connection at least once will the reconnection logic kick in.

Once the client has successfully established the TCP connection, sent the CONNECT and the first PING protocols, and received the corresponding PONG, the client will be in the CONNECTED state.

Customizing a Connection

In the Go client, the Connect function uses the *variadic options* technique, which has become popular among the Go community[1] to customize the connection. Listing 3-3 shows how to set a label to identify the client by using the nats.Name option function on connect.

Listing 3-3. Setting a Name Label to a Client

```
package main

import (
        "log"
        "runtime"

        "github.com/nats io/go-nats"
)

func main() {
        nc, err := nats.Connect("nats://127.0.0.1:4222",
                nats.Name("practical-nats-client"),
        )
        if err != nil {
                log.Fatalf("Error: %s", err)
        }
```

---

[1]"Functional Options for Friendly APIs" by Dave Cheney https://dave.cheney. net/2014/10/17/functional-options-for-friendly-apis

```
        nc.Subscribe("greeting", func(m *nats.Msg) {
                log.Printf("[Received] %s", string(m.Data))
        })
        nc.Publish("greeting", []byte("hello world"))
        runtime.Goexit()
}
```

Then, the client on a successfully established connection will announce the name of the connection to the server via the CONNECT command (see Listing 3-4).

Listing 3-4. Sending Metadata via the CONNECT Protocol

```
CONNECT {...,"name":"practical-nats-client","lang":"go",
"version":"1.3.1"}
```

Setting a name for the connection can be useful for monitoring purposes, as this information will now be displayed in the monitoring endpoint from the NATS Server. The NATS Server monitoring endpoint can be activated by using the -m flag (see Listing 3-5), and it is customarily set to use the port 8222.

Listing 3-5. Enabling the Monitoring Endpoint from the Server

```
gnatsd -m 8222
```

Then if an HTTP request is made to the 8222 port, it is possible to inspect the current state of clients connected to the system (see Listing 3-6).

Listing 3-6. Retrieving Client Information via a NATS Monitoring Port

```
curl http://127.0.0.1:8222/connz
...
{
  "now": "2018-01-03T21:33:26.977883-08:00",
  "num_connections": 1,
```

```
"total": 1,
"offset": 0,
"limit": 1024,
"connections": [
  {
    "cid": 1,
    "ip": "127.0.0.1",
    "port": 56721,
    "start": "2018-01-03T21:33:24.354268-08:00",
    "last_activity": "2018-01-03T21:33:24.355002-08:00",
    "uptime": "2s",
    "idle": "2s",
    "pending_bytes": 0,
    "in_msgs": 1,
    "out_msgs": 1,
    "in_bytes": 11,
    "out_bytes": 11,
    "subscriptions": 1,
    "name": "practical-nats-client",
    "lang": "go",
    "version": "1.3.1"
  }
]
}
```

As you can see, the client has announced the lang and version of the client, which can be helpful to identify the type of client that is currently connected to the server. Tools like nats-top use this monitoring endpoint and show this metadata in order to support inspecting the current state from a server. Monitoring the NATS Server will be covered in more detail in another chapter.

Authorization Credentials

The NATS Server has a notion of authorization groups and users, which can be used to increase security of the server. In order to identify a client, CONNECT plays an important here, as it shows how a client can set the user password or an auth token in order to identify the server.

We can use the -user and -pass flags from the server to set a single pair of credentials to be used by all the clients (see Listing 3-7).

Listing 3-7. Setting User and Pass Authorization in the Server

```
gnatsd -m 8222 -user foo -pass secret
```

Then, from the client, we can set these via the connect options (see Listing 3-8).

Listing 3-8. Setting User Credentials

```
package main

import (
        "log"
        "runtime"

        "github.com/nats-io/go-nats"
)

func main() {
        nc, err := nats.Connect("nats://127.0.0.1:4222",
                nats.UserInfo("foo", "secret"),
        )
        if err != nil {
                log.Fatalf("Error: %s", err)
        }
```

```
nc.Subscribe("greeting", func(m *nats.Msg) {
        log.Printf("[Received] %s", string(m.Data))
    })
    nc.Publish("greeting", []byte("hello world"))
    runtime.Goexit()
}
```

Then the client will send one CONNECT (see Listing 3-9).

Listing 3-9. Retrieving Client Information via a NATS Monitoring Port

```
CONNECT {...,"user":"foo","pass":"secret",...}
```

After that, the connection will be successfully established; otherwise, if the client has the wrong credentials an -ERR 'Authorization Violation' protocol error will be sent to the client before the server closes the connection.

If an authorization timeout is set in the server and the client does not authenticate fast enough, the server will send an -ERR 'Authorization Timeout' protocol error and close the connection as well.

Using Publish and Subscribe

The Publish and Subscribe APIs are how the NATS clients publish and receive messages respectively, internally leveraging the PUB and SUB commands from the protocol. A simple example of publishing and receiving messages is shown in Listing 3-10.

Listing 3-10. Publish/Subscribe with the NATS Client

```go
package main

import (
        "log"
        "runtime"

        "github.com/nats-io/go-nats"
)

func main() {
        nc, err := nats.Connect("nats://127.0.0.1:4222",
                nats.UserInfo("foo", "secret"),
        )
        if err != nil {
                log.Fatalf("Error: %s", err)
        }
        nc.Subscribe("greeting", func(m *nats.Msg) {
                log.Printf("[Received] %s", string(m.Data))
        })
        nc.Publish("greeting", []byte("hello world"))
        runtime.Goexit()
}
```

Using Publish

Publish takes the subject where the message will be sent (greetings) and a
payload in bytes. The payload sent to the server is opaque to the server; there
is no extra encoding/decoding required by the server. Users of the client
libraries are free to use whichever encoder library they see fit. We could use
JSON to add some metadata to the message being sent. Listing 3-11 shows
an example program doing this and Listing 3-12 shows an example result of
running it.

Listing 3-11. Using a Custom JSON Encoder/Decoder

```go
package main

import (
        "encoding/json"
        "log"
        "runtime"

        "github.com/nats-io/go-nats"
)

func main() {
        nc, err := nats.Connect("nats://127.0.0.1:4222",
                nats.UserInfo("foo", "secret"),
        )
        if err != nil {
                log.Fatalf("Error: %s", err)
        }
        nc.Subscribe("greeting", func(m *nats.Msg) {
                log.Printf("[Received] %s", string(m.Data))
        })

        payload := struct {
                RequestID string
                Data      []byte
        }{
                RequestID: "1234-5678-90",
                Data:      []byte("encoded data"),
        }
        msg, err := json.Marshal(payload)
        if err != nil {
                log.Fatalf("Error: %s", err)
        }
```

```
    nc.Publish("greeting", msg)
    runtime.Goexit()
}
```

Listing 3-12. Running the Program

```
$ go run basic-pub-sub-json.go
2018/01/04 23:23:01 [Received] {"RequestID":"1234-5678-
90","Data":"ZW5jb2RlZCBkYXRh"}
```

The Go NATS client has built-in support for encoders and decoders too; these are covered in another chapter.

Using Subscribe

The Subscribe API is how the client registers interest in a subject. Depending on the client, there may be multiple APIs available for controlling how the messages will be consumed. The Go NATS client, for example, has three variations of the API: Subscribe, ChanSubscribe, and SubscribeSync.

In the NATS clients, the Subscribe method usually takes a callback that's invoked by the client library as the NATS Server delivers messages to the client. Compare for example the same API in the Go (see Listing 3-13), Ruby (see Listing 3-14), and Node.js (see Listing 3-15) clients.

Listing 3-13. Subscribing in Go

```
// Go
nc.Subscribe("foo", func(m *nats.Msg) {
        log.Println("[Received]: " + string(m.Data))
})
```

Listing 3-14. Subscribing in Ruby

```ruby
# Ruby
nats.subscribe("foo") do |msg|
  puts "[Received]: #{msg}"
end
```

Listing 3-15. Subscribing in Node.js

```js
# Node.js
nats.subscribe('foo', function(msg) {
  console.log('[Received]: ' + msg);
});
```

Something very important to note about the behavior from a subscription is that, for a single subscription, only a single message will be handled at a time sequentially, *not in parallel.* If we have multiple subscriptions and one of them is processing messages slower than the rest, this will not affect the other subscriptions. Listing 3-16 shows an example where there are a couple of subscriptions, one on a bare subject and another one on a wildcard.

Listing 3-16. Head of Line Blocking Example

```go
package main

import (
        "log"
        "runtime"
        "time"

        "github.com/nats-io/go-nats"
)
```

```go
func main() {
        nc, err := nats.Connect("nats://127.0.0.1:4222",
                nats.UserInfo("foo", "secret"),
        )
        if err != nil {
                log.Fatalf("Error: %s", err)
        }
        nc.Subscribe("greeting", func(m *nats.Msg) {
                log.Printf("[Received] %s", string(m.Data))
        })
        nc.Subscribe(">", func(m *nats.Msg) {
                log.Printf("[Wildcard] %s", string(m.Data))
                time.Sleep(1 * time.Second)
        })

        for i := 0; i < 10; i++ {
                nc.Publish("greeting", []byte("hello world!"))
        }
        runtime.Goexit()
}
```

The result from running Listing 3-16 can be found in Listing 3-17. Note how the messages from the wildcard subscriptions are delayed more than those from the bare subscription.

Listing 3-17. Head of Line Blocking Occurs Only for the Same Subscription

```
2018/01/04 23:43:03 [Wildcard] hello world!
2018/01/04 23:43:03 [Received] hello world!
2018/01/04 23:43:03 [Received] hello world!
2018/01/04 23:43:03 [Received] hello world!
2018/01/04 23:43:03 [Received] hello world!
2018/01/04 23:43:03 [Received] hello world!
```

```
2018/01/04 23:43:03 [Received] hello world!
2018/01/04 23:43:03 [Received] hello world!
2018/01/04 23:43:03 [Received] hello world!
2018/01/04 23:43:03 [Received] hello world!
2018/01/04 23:43:03 [Received] hello world!
2018/01/04 23:43:04 [Wildcard] hello world!
2018/01/04 23:43:05 [Wildcard] hello world!
2018/01/04 23:43:06 [Wildcard] hello world!
2018/01/04 23:43:07 [Wildcard] hello world!
2018/01/04 23:43:08 [Wildcard] hello world!
2018/01/04 23:43:09 [Wildcard] hello world!
2018/01/04 23:43:10 [Wildcard] hello world!
2018/01/04 23:43:11 [Wildcard] hello world!
2018/01/04 23:43:12 [Wildcard] hello world!
```

Using QueueSubscribe

The QueueSubscribe API works pretty much the same as the Subscribe
API counterpart (and in the case of the Go client, has the same other
variations). The only difference is that it creates a distributed queue group
to which the server will be balancing requests randomly. Listing 3-18
shows an example of creating a workers queue on the greetings subject.

Listing 3-18. Using QueueSubscribe in Go

```go
package main

import (
        "log"
        "runtime"

        "github.com/nats-io/go-nats"
)
```

```
func main() {
        nc, err := nats.Connect("nats://127.0.0.1:4222")
        if err != nil {
                log.Fatalf("Error: %s", err)
        }
        nc.QueueSubscribe("greeting", "workers", func(m *nats.
        Msg) {
                log.Printf("[Received] %s", string(m.Data))
        })
        nc.Publish("greeting", []byte("hello world!!!"))
        runtime.Goexit()
}
```

In Listing 3-19, it shown what the client internally will be sending to the server. As we covered in the previous chapter, this will result in creating a load balanced subscription.

Listing 3-19. Protocol Sent from QueueSubscribe

```
SUB greeting workers 1
```

Removing a Subscription

In order to remove interest in a subscription, in the Go NATS client, the Subscribe call returns a Subscription type that allows the library user to control how many messages to receive or whether to stop receiving altogether. In Listing 3-20, the client will only receive five messages, even though the client is publishing 10 in total.

Listing 3-20. Unsubscribing in Go

```go
package main

import (
        "log"
        "runtime"

        "github.com/nats-io/go-nats"
)

func main() {
        nc, err := nats.Connect("nats://127.0.0.1:4222")
        if err != nil {
                log.Fatalf("Error: %s", err)
        }
        sub, err := nc.Subscribe("greeting", func(m *nats.Msg) {
                log.Printf("[Received] %s", string(m.Data))
        })
        if err != nil {
                log.Fatalf("Error: %s", err)
        }
        sub.AutoUnsubscribe(5)

        for i := 0; i < 10; i++ {
                nc.Publish("greeting", []byte("hello world!!!"))
        }
        runtime.Goexit()
}
```

To remove interest instantly on a subject, we call Unsubscribe on the
Subscription type. In Listing 3-21, very few messages will be received.

Listing 3-21. Unsubscribing in Go

```go
package main

import (
        "log"
        "runtime"

        "github.com/nats-io/go-nats"
)

func main() {
        nc, err := nats.Connect("nats://127.0.0.1:4222")
        if err != nil {
                log.Fatalf("Error: %s", err)
        }
        sub, err := nc.Subscribe("greeting", func(m *nats.Msg) {
                log.Printf("[Received] %s", string(m.Data))
        })
        if err != nil {
                log.Fatalf("Error: %s", err)
        }

        for i := 0; i < 5; i++ {
                nc.Publish("greeting", []byte("hello world!!!"))
        }
         nc.Flush()

        // Remove subscription
        sub.Unsubscribe()
```

```
for i := 0; i < 5; i++ {
        nc.Publish("greeting", []byte("hello world!!!"))
}

runtime.Goexit()
}
```

Note that it is possible also to unsubscribe directly from the message callback. When doing so, you have the guarantee that the callback will not be invoked again, even if there were messages internally that would have been dispatched otherwise. An example of this usage is found in Listing 3-22.

Listing 3-22. Unsubscribing From Within Subscribe Callback

```
package main

import (
        "log"
        "runtime"

        "github.com/nats-io/go-nats"
)

func main() {
        nc, err := nats.Connect("nats://127.0.0.1:4222")
        if err != nil {
                log.Fatalf("Error: %s", err)
        }

        var counter int
        var sub *nats.Subscription
        sub, err = nc.Subscribe("greeting", func(m *nats.Msg) {
                log.Printf("[Received] %s", string(m.Data))
                // Remove subscription after receiving a couple
                // of messages.
```

```
                counter++
                if counter == 2 {
                        sub.Unsubscribe()
                }
        })
        if err != nil {
                log.Fatalf("Error: %s", err)
        }

        for i := 0; i < 5; i++ {
                nc.Publish("greeting", []byte("hello world!!!"))
        }
        nc.Flush()

        runtime.Goexit()
}
```

Using Flush

The Flush API is very convenient in the NATS clients, as it provides the user with a method to be able to control behavior from the client to act in a more synchronous way. Listing 3-23 shows an example of a client with 10 messages and then calling Flush(), which would ensure that the server has received the first 10 messages before then sending another message.

Listing 3-23. Flushing the Buffer in Go

```
package main

import (
        "log"
        "runtime"

        "github.com/nats-io/go-nats"
)
```

```go
func main() {
        nc, err := nats.Connect("nats://127.0.0.1:4222")
        if err != nil {
                log.Fatalf("Error: %s", err)
        }
        nc.Subscribe("greeting", func(m *nats.Msg) {
                log.Printf("[Received] %s", string(m.Data))
        })

        for i := 0; i < 10; i++ {
                nc.Publish("greeting", []byte("hello world!!!"))
        }
        nc.Flush()

        err = nc.Publish("greeting", []byte("hello world!!!"))
        if err != nil {
                log.Fatalf("Error: %s", err)
        }

        runtime.Goexit()
}
```

Internally what it does is send everything that has accumulated in the pending buffer from the client. Then, it sends a PING to the server, and then waits for the PONG. As soon as the client receives the PONG reply, the Flush call will unblock and let the client assume that the messages that were fired have been processed by the server.

Using Request

The Request API enables the client to publish a message and then wait for someone to reply. A simple example of the Request/Response functionality from NATS can be found in Listing 3-24, with the result of running the program shown in Listing 3-25.

Listing 3-24. Request/Response in the Go NATS Client

```go
package main

import (
        "log"
        "time"

        "github.com/nats-io/go-nats"
)

func main() {
        nc, err := nats.Connect("nats://127.0.0.1:4222")
        if err != nil {
                log.Fatalf("Error: %s", err)
        }
        nc.Subscribe("help", func(m *nats.Msg) {
                log.Printf("[Received]: %s", string(m.Data))
                nc.Publish(m.Reply, []byte("I can help!!!"))
        })
        response, err := nc.Request("help", []byte("help!!"),
        1*time.Second)
        if err != nil {
                log.Fatalf("Error: %s", err)
        }
        log.Println("[Response]: " + string(response.Data))
}
```

Listing 3-25. Running the Program

```
2018/01/05 00:27:27 [Received]: help!!
2018/01/05 00:27:27 [Response]: I can help!!!
```

Internally, the Request API uses unique inboxes for each request, which are then announced to the server.

As of recent releases, there are two versions of the Request/Response implementation, we'll call these the classic and new style Request/Response.

The Classic Request/Response

For a long time, the NATS clients used the ephemeral subscriptions in order to achieve 1:1 communications. Listing 3-26 shows how the Request/Response originally worked.

Listing 3-26. Request/Response Protocol with UNSUB

```
# Unique subscription using sid: 2
SUB _INBOX.1GlZMJXHYj9Wkmdu7ugvpF  2

# Limit to receive a single response
UNSUB 2 1

# Publish the message on help subject using unique subscription
PUB help  INBOX.1GlZMJXHYj9Wkmdu7ugvpF 6
help!!

# Received response
MSG _INBOX.1GlZMJXHYj9Wkmdu7ugvpF 2 13
I can help!!!
```

One of the limitations from that implementation is that it heavily used subscriptions, which induces more overhead to the NATS clustering implementation, as the subscriptions had to be propagated per request. On the other hand, this implementation has the benefit of guaranteeing that the client will only receive a single response (since it was expressed via UNSUB that only a single message is desired).

In the NATS Go client, this mode can still be activated by using the nats.UseOldRequestStyle option (see Listing 3-27).

Listing 3-27. Old Style Request/Response in the Go NATS Client

```
package main

import (
        "log"
        "time"

        "github.com/nats-io/go-nats"
)

func main() {
        nc, err := nats.Connect("nats://127.0.0.1:4222",
                nats.UseOldRequestStyle(),
        )
        if err != nil {
                log.Fatalf("Error: %s", err)
        }
        nc.Subscribe("help", func(m *nats.Msg) {
                log.Printf("[Received]: %s", string(m.Data))
                nc.Publish(m.Reply, []byte("I can help!!!"))
        })
        response, err := nc.Request("help", []byte("help!!"),
        1*time.Second)
        if err != nil {
                log.Fatalf("Error: %s", err)
        }
        log.Println("[Response]: " + string(response.Data))
}
```

The New Style Request/Response

As of recent releases, the NATS team has been moving to a new style of doing Request/Response, where the client library creates a single wildcard subscription once per connection solely for this purpose. Listing 3-28 shows how the Request/Response protocol was reworked to be less chatty over the network.

Listing 3-28. New Style Request/Response Protocol

```
# Create single subscription for requests with wildcard handler
SUB _INBOX.9erElxb6mQiE7VUkfygPEL.*  2

# Publish requests inbox plus another unique subject
PUB help _INBOX.9erElxb6mQiE7VUkfygPEL.9erElxb6mQiE7VUkfygPIE 6
help!!

# Receives response which was sent to long unique subject
MSG _INBOX.9erElxb6mQiE7VUkfygPEL.9erElxb6mQiE7VUkfygPIE 2 13
I can help!!!
```

One of the benefits of this approach is that it means less work for the server as a single subscription is used instead of several. On the other hand, it means that when N is very large, the client will receive multiple responses that it needs to drop (since UNSUB is not being used). However, in combination with QueueSubscribe, it works really well since it means that a single subscriber will receive the message and send the response back.

A Note on Asynchronous I/O

Something that's common to all the implementations of the NATS client is that they work asynchronously under the hood. In the previous chapter, we saw that in order to publish a message, you can send bytes (see Listing 3-29).

Listing 3-29. Sending Five Bytes with PUB

```
PUB hello 5\r\n
world\r\n
```

In the clients, the same can be done using the Go client (see Listing 3-30).

Listing 3-30. Publishing a Message in the Go Client

```
package main

import (
        "log"
        "github.com/nats-io/go-nats"
)

func main(){
        nc, err := nats.Connect("nats://127.0.0.1:4222")
        if err != nil {
                log.Fatalf("Error: %s", err)
        }
        nc.Publish("hello", []byte("world"))
}
```

But if we try running this program, the program may exit so fast that the message would not actually be sent to the server. This is because the Publish API is *non-blocking* and what has actually occurred is that the world payload has been placed in the pending buffer from the client, and then eventually is published.

In order to ensure that the message will be sent in this program, the Flush API from the client can be used to ensure that everything has been sent and processed by the server (see Listing 3-31).

Listing 3-31. Publish Then Flush in the Go Client

```
package main

import (
        "log"

        "github.com/nats-io/go-nats"
)

func main() {
        nc, err := nats.Connect("nats://127.0.0.1:4222")
        if err != nil {
                log.Fatalf("Error: %s", err)
        }
        nc.Publish("hello", []byte("world"))
        nc.Flush()
}
```

This issue often comes up with new NATS users, when they're trying to benchmark how fast a client receives messages to a subscription under a publishing tight loop without relinquishing control to process the messages that are being delivered. This issue is replicated in the example shown in Listing 3-32.

Listing 3-32. Slow Consumer Example with the Go Client

```
package main

import (
        "log"

        "github.com/nats-io/go-nats"
)
```

```go
func main() {
        nc, err := nats.Connect(nats.DefaultURL)
        if err != nil {
                log.Fatalf("Error: %s", err)
        }
        msg := []byte("Hello World!")
        nc.Subscribe("greetings", func(_ *nats.Msg) {})
        for i := 0; i < 100000000; i++ {
                nc.Publish("greetings", msg)
        }
}
```

The resultant server output after running the previous program is shown in Listing 3-33. Note that in the server, we would find at least one Slow Consumer Detected error.

Listing 3-33. Resulting Server Output

```
[23187] 2018/01/07 19:02:54.408540 [INF] Starting nats-server
version 1.0.4
[23187] 2018/01/07 19:02:54.408810 [INF] Listening for client
connections on 127.0.0.1:4222
[23187] 2018/01/07 19:02:54.408819 [INF] Server is ready
[23187] 2018/01/07 19:02:59.454415 [INF] 127.0.0.1:62079 -
cid:1 - Slow Consumer Detected
```

With the exception of Request and Flush, which both block until receiving a response from the server, all other APIs that use the protocol *do not block* and work asynchronously.

Another issue to keep in mind is that the error handling has to be done asynchronously as well. For example, the subject name _SYS is reserved for future use by the system, so trying to send something to the subject is going to result in a permissions violation error. Listing 3-34 shows an example of receiving an error asynchronously that will not close the connection, and Listing 3-35 shows the result of running it.

Listing 3-34. Permissions Violation async Error

```go
package main

import (
        "log"
        "time"

        "github.com/nats-io/go-nats"
)

func main() {
        nc, err := nats.Connect(nats.DefaultURL,
                nats.ErrorHandler(func(
                        _ *nats.Conn,
                        _ *nats.Subscription,
                        err error,
                ) {
                        log.Printf("Async Error: %s", err)
                }))
        if err != nil {
                log.Fatalf("Error: %s", err)
        }
        nc.Publish("_SYS.hi", []byte("hi"))
        nc.Flush()
        time.Sleep(1 * time.Second)
}
```

Listing 3-35. Running a Program with the Permissions Violation Error

```
2018/01/07 20:02:35 Async Error: nats: permissions violation
for publish to "_sys.hi"
```

The clients also offer an API called LastError, which captures the error protocol responses sent by the server, so in the case of the previous example, we can do something similar, as shown in Listing 3-36.

Listing 3-36. Using LastError to Retrieve Past Errors

```go
package main

import (
        "log"
        "time"

        "github.com/nats-io/go-nats"
)

func main() {
        nc, err := nats.Connect(nats.DefaultURL)
        if err != nil {
                log.Fatalf("Error: %s", err)
        }
        nc.Publish("_SYS.hi", []byte("hi"))
        nc.Flush()
        time.Sleep(1 * time.Second)
        log.Printf("Last Error: %s", nc.LastError())
}
```

States of a NATS Connection

The ideal state from a connection to NATS is to be connected to the system (remember, NATS is intended to act as a dial tone after all). Table 3-2 lists and describes the states from a NATS connection and Figure 3-1 shows the state transitions of a NATS connection.

Table 3-2. *The NATS Client API*

State	Description
CONNECTING	First attempt to try to connect to NATS
CONNECTED	Connection to NATS is healthy
RECONNECTING	Retrying to establish connection
DISCONNECTED	Just disconnected from NATS
CLOSED	Client connection is now forever closed

In order to be able to send and receive messages, a client has to be in the CONNECTED state. Whenever there is a disconnection to a server, the NATS client will attempt to connect to another server in the cluster pool for a certain number of times (the RECONNECTING and DISCONNECTED states), after which it will give up trying to connect and reach the CLOSED state.

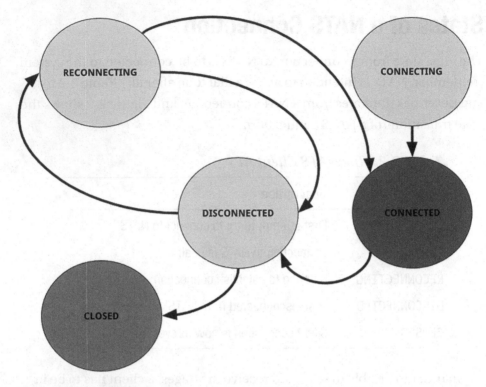

Figure 3-1. *State transitions from a NATS connection*

While a client is reconnecting, if the client tries to publish or subscribe, the client will not necessarily receive an error telling it that it failed to send the message because it is not connected. This is because of the internal asynchronous engine from the client, which will buffer the commands onto a pending buffer. In the case of the Go NATS client, this buffer is going to be 8MB (customizable via the `ReconnectBufSize` option when connecting).

Listing 3-37 shows an example of a component in a system that periodically publishes data, which is a very common way of using NATS. After this pending buffer is exhausted, the calls will error out.

Listing 3-37. Limiting the Size of the Reconnect Buffer

```go
package main

import (
        "log"
        "time"

        "github.com/nats-io/go-nats"
)

func main() {
         opts := nats.DefaultOptions

        // Arbitrarily small reconnecting buffer
        opts.ReconnectBufSize = 256
        nc, err := opts.Connect()
        if err != nil {
                log.Fatalf("Error: %s", err)
        }

        for range time.NewTicker(500 * time.Millisecond).C {
                // If disconnected for too long and buffer is
                  full
                // then the client will receive a synchronous
                  error.
                err := nc.Publish("numbers", []byte("4 8 15 16
                23 42"))
                if err != nil {
                        // nats: outbound buffer limit exceeded
                        log.Fatalf("Error: %s", err)
                }
        }
}
```

Depending on the case, we might not want the buffered data accumulated during a reconnection to be flushed to the server (since it might be stale) and will publish only when the client is connected. For these use cases, we can check the current state of the connection and skip it or give up altogether in case the connection to NATS has been closed or is reconnecting. An example of this usage is found in Listing 3-38.

Listing 3-38. Skipping Sending Messages During Reconnecting Events

```go
package main

import (
        "log"
        "time"

        "github.com/nats-io/go-nats"
)

func main() {
        nc, err := nats.Connect(nats.DefaultURL)
        if err != nil {
                log.Fatalf("Error: %s", err)
        }
        for range time.NewTicker(500 * time.Millisecond).C {
                if nc.IsClosed() {
                        log.Fatalf("Disconnected forever!
                        Exiting...")
                }
                if nc.IsReconnecting() {
                        log.Println("Disconnected temporarily,
                        skipping for now...")
                        continue
                }
```

```
        err := nc.Publish("numbers", []byte("4 8 15 16
        23 42"))
        if err != nil {
                // nats: outbound buffer limit exceeded
                log.Fatalf("Error: %s", err)
        }
    }
}
```

Clients Reconnection Logic

As previously mentioned, the available NATS clients all have client reconnection enabled by default. There are a number of customizations that can be done to the reconnection logic via Connect options. For example, in order to make the client never stop reconnecting, we can set the maximum number attempts to -1 so that it never stops retrying. Listing 3-39 shows how to tell the client to never stop reconnecting.

Listing 3-39. Setting the Client to Always Try to Reconnect

```
package main

import (
        "log"
        "time"

        "github.com/nats-io/go-nats"
)

func main() {
        nc, err := nats.Connect(nats.DefaultURL, nats.
        MaxReconnects(-1))
```

```
        if err != nil {
                log.Fatalf("Error: %s", err)
        }

        // If disconnected for too long and buffer is full
        // then the client will receive a synchronous error.
        for range time.NewTicker(1 * time.Second).C {
                err := nc.Publish("hello", []byte("world"))
                if err != nil {
                        log.Printf("Error: %s", err)
                }
        }
}
```

Depending on the case, we may to disconnect and disable reconnecting altogether. Listing 3-40 shows an example of how to do this.

Listing 3-40. Disabling the Reconnect Logic and Bailing on Disconnect

```
package main

import (
        "log"
        "time"

        "github.com/nats-io/go-nats"
)

func main() {
        nc, err := nats.Connect("nats://127.0.0.1:4222",
        nats.NoReconnect())
        if err != nil {
                log.Fatalf("Error: %s", err)
        }
```

```
        // Since we disallow reconnection, this should report
        // an error quickly after stopping the NATS Server.
        for range time.NewTicker(1 * time.Second).C {
                err := nc.Publish("hello", []byte("world"))
                if err != nil {
                        log.Fatalf("Error: %s", err)
                }
        }
}
```

Once it's reconnected, we can expect the client to replay any present subscription that may have been done by the client, as well as flush any pending command that may have been published during the service interruption to the NATS Server. If we are running Listing 3-41, which will always reconnect and then restart a NATS Server, we will see that the client will continue to receive the published hello messages.

Listing 3-41. Subscriptions Are Restored on Reconnect

```
package main

import (
        "log"
        "time"

        "github.com/nats-io/go-nats"
)

func main() {
        nc, err := nats.Connect(nats.DefaultURL,
        nats.MaxReconnects(-1))
        if err != nil {
                log.Fatalf("Error: %s", err)
        }
```

```
    nc.Subscribe("hello", func(m *nats.Msg) {
        log.Printf("[Received] %s", string(m.Data))
    })

    nc.Subscribe("*", func(m *nats.Msg) {
        log.Printf("[Wildcard] %s", string(m.Data))
    })
    for range time.NewTicker(1 * time.Second).C {
        err := nc.Publish("hello", []byte("hello
        world"))
        if err != nil {
            log.Printf("Error: %s", err)
        }
    }
}
```

Event Callbacks

As the clients handle the protocol asynchronously, there are a number of
events callbacks on which we can rely in order to be aware of what is going
on with the NATS connection.

Most clients offer at least asynchronous event callbacks for when a
connection is disconnected, reconnected, and closed, plus callbacks to
handle asynchronous events. Newer clients (and if connected to newer
NATS Servers) also provide a callback to be invoked when a server joins
the NATS cluster. Listing 3-42 shows an example of the latest version of the
Go client setting callbacks for all possible events.

Listing 3-42. Example Event Callbacks from the Client

```go
package main

import (
        "log"
        "time"

        "github.com/nats-io/go-nats"
)

func main() {
        nc, err := nats.Connect(nats.DefaultURL,
                nats.DisconnectHandler(func(nc *nats.Conn) {
                        log.Printf("Disconnected!\n")
                }),
                nats.ReconnectHandler(func(nc *nats.Conn) {
                        log.Printf("Reconnected to %v!\n",
                        nc.ConnectedUrl())
                }),
                nats.ClosedHandler(func(nc *nats.Conn) {
                        log.Printf("Connection closed. Reason:
                        %q\n", nc.LastError())
                }),
                nats.DiscoveredServersHandler(func(nc *nats.
                Conn) {
                        log.Printf("Server discovered\n")
                }),
                nats.ErrorHandler(func(
                        _ *nats.Conn,
                        _ *nats.Subscription,
                        err error,
                ) {
```

```
                           log.Printf("Async Error: %s", err)
                }),
        )
        if err != nil {
                log.Fatalf("Error: %s", err)
        }

        nc.Subscribe("hello", func(m *nats.Msg) {
                log.Printf("[Received] %s", string(m.Data))
        })
        for range time.NewTicker(1 * time.Second).C {
                err := nc.Publish("hello", []byte("hello
                world"))
                if err != nil {
                        log.Printf("Error: %s", err)
                }
        }
}
```

Using Close

The Close API terminates the connection to NATS forever, never trying
to reconnect again. If the client had been connected to a NATS Server
and Close is called, then it will reach the CLOSED state, after which the
client will not be able to reconnect further. Once Close is called, all API
commands from the client will fail with a nats: connection closed error
(see Listing 3-43).

Listing 3-43. Using Close to Wrap Up Connection to NATS

```go
package main

import (
        "log"
        "runtime"

        "github.com/nats-io/go-nats"
)

func main() {
        nc, err := nats.Connect("nats://127.0.0.1:4222")
        if err != nil {
                log.Fatalf("Error: %s", err)
        }
        nc.Subscribe("greeting", func(m *nats.Msg) {
                log.Printf("[Received] %s", string(m.Data))
        })

        for i := 0; i < 10; i++ {
                nc.Publish("greeting", []byte("hello world!!!"))
        }
        nc.Flush()

        // Terminate connection to NATS
        nc.Close()

        // Error: nats: connection closed
        err = nc.Publish("greeting", []byte("hello world!!!"))
        if err != nil {
                log.Fatalf("Error: %s", err)
        }

        runtime.Goexit()
}
```

When calling Close, the NATS clients, before terminating the connection, also try to flush anything that was in the internal pending buffer before terminating the connection. If the NATS client is used in a batch-like program where some data is published and then stops running, it is recommended that you use Close to gracefully close the NATS connection and flush any data that was pending before exiting.

Summary

In this chapter, we saw some of the important usability aspects to consider about the NATS clients and how they behave, so we should have better foundations for the next chapters, where we will be building a sample application using the Go client. Before tackling that, we take a closer look at the features from the server and then look at its clustering implementation in order to achieve high availability.

CHAPTER 4

Setting Up NATS

In Chapter 2, we saw that it is fairly straightforward to get a NATS Server
up and running, as there are not many knobs required when we're just
sticking to the defaults.

In this chapter, we will take a further look at the different configuration
parameters from the server, both from the command line and as part of the
custom configuration file format from the server.

Furthermore, the NATS team provides binaries for most of the popular
OS architectures on each release, as well as curating official images for
Docker. This makes it easier to work with container orchestration systems.
We also cover how Docker works in this chapter.

Server Configuration

The NATS Server takes little configuration and has good defaults overall,
so not a lot is required to configure it. The server can be configured just
by using the command line, which is useful in cloud-native deployments
and container orchestration systems, where it is common to just set all the
options inline as part of a manifest or by using a configuration file. As it is
with most programs, you can see a list of all the available options via the -h
or --help flag (shown in Listing 4-1).

© Waldemar Quevedo 2018
W. Quevedo, *Practical NATS*, https://doi.org/10.1007/978-1-4842-3570-6_4

Listing 4-1. Help Message from gnatsd

```
$ gnatsd --help

Usage: gnatsd [options]

Server Options:
    -a, --addr <host>          Bind to host address (default:
                               0.0.0.0)
    -p, --port <port>          Use port for clients (default:
                               4222)
    -P, --pid <file>           File to store PID
    -m, --http_port <port>     Use port for http monitoring
    -ms,--https_port <port>    Use port for https monitoring
    -c, --config <file>        Configuration file
```

To configure the server by using a configuration file, we can use the -c, --config flag. Listing 4-2 shows how to modify the port used by the clients to connect using the configuration file.

Listing 4-2. Using a Config File from gnatsd

```
cat << EOF > /tmp/nats.conf
listen = 0.0.0.0:4333

# Disable showing time in the logs
logtime = false
EOF

$ gnatsd --config /tmp/nats.conf

[41594] [INF] Starting nats-server version 1.1.0
[41594] [INF] Listening for client connections on 0.0.0.0:4333
[41594] [INF] Server is ready
```

Keep in mind that the options set in the command line override anything that is present in the configuration file. Listing 4-3 shows how the command-line option value -p 4444 overrides the value from the configuration file, which is 4333.

Listing 4-3. Using a Config File from gnatsd

```
cat << EOF > /tmp/nats.conf
listen = 0.0.0.0:4333

# Disable showing time in the logs
logtime = false
EOF

$ gnatsd -p 4444 --config /tmp/nats.conf

[41594] [INF] Starting nats-server version 1.1.0
[41594] [INF] Listening for client connections on 0.0.0.0:4444
[41594] [INF] Server is ready
```

NATS has its own custom configuration format, which is inspired in part by the configuration format from Nginx and a bit by JSON as well (it is actually a superset of JSON, although unlike JSON, it does support comments). You may recognize some of these ideas from other configuration formats projects, such as the UCL configuration format (https://github.com/vstakhov/libucl) or HCL from Hashicorp (https://github.com/hashicorp/hcl), though the style from the configuration format from NATS Server predates both of those referenced implementations. It was introduced circa 2012. You can find more about the syntax of the configuration file in the section at the end of this chapter.

In the next section, we look at each of the knobs exposed by the server and show how to configure them via the command line and the configuration file.

Exposed Ports

There are three main ports that a production gnatsd server will expose: the port to which clients will be connecting, the port used for clustering, and the monitoring port. Figure 4-1 shows a three-node cluster to which clients are connecting on port 4222, nodes adding each other as peers by using port 6222, and also an HTTP client fetching metrics by connecting to port 8222.

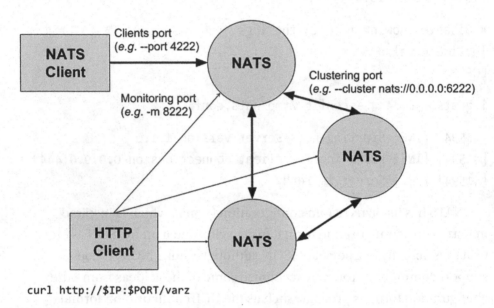

Figure 4-1. *Ports used by gnatsd*

By default, the client will only be listening for clients connecting on port 4222 (see Listing 4-4). The Docker image differs a bit here and exposes all these ports; see more on that in the Docker section in this chapter.

Listing 4-4. Starting gnatsd with the Default Options

```
$ gnatsd
[42532] 2018/03/26 20:37:09.142239 [INF] Starting nats-server
version 1.1.0
[42532] 2018/03/26 20:37:09.142545 [INF] Listening for client
connections on 0.0.0.0:4222
[42532] 2018/03/26 20:37:09.142555 [INF] Server is ready
```

The port can be customized with the -p (or --port) flag. By default, it will bind to 0.0.0.0, but this can be overridden via -a (or --addr). Listing 4-5 shows how to bind the server to localhost only on a different port.

Listing 4-5. Customizing Port and Bind from the Server

```
$ gnatsd -p 4333 -a 127.0.0.1

[42685] 2018/01/21 20:53:00.028903 [INF] Starting nats-server
version 1.0.4
[42685] 2018/01/21 20:53:00.029384 [INF] Listening for client
connections on 127.0.0.1:4333
[42685] 2018/01/21 20:53:00.029398 [INF] Server is ready
```

The monitoring port exposes an HTTP endpoint from which it is possible to gather data about the running stats from the server. By default, it is not exposed (although it is in the NATS Docker image). We can set a port for the monitoring endpoint to use via the -m (or --http_port) flag (see Listing 4-6).

Listing 4-6. Setting up the monitoring endpoint from the server

```
$ gnatsd -logtime=false -m 8222 &

[43310] [INF] Starting nats-server version 1.0.4
[43310] [INF] Starting http monitor on 0.0.0.0:8222
[43310] [INF] Listening for client connections on 0.0.0.0:4222
[43310] [INF] Server is ready
```

```
$ curl http://127.0.0.1:8222/varz
{
"server_id": "rvhJFnzYVL6a3tBk96lf65",
...
  "start": "2018-01-21T21:23:31.343454-08:00",
  "now": "2018-01-21T21:24:46.933616-08:00",
  "uptime": "1m15s",
  "mem": 8962048,
  "cores": 4,
  "cpu": 0,
  "connections": 0,
  "total_connections": 0,
  "routes": 0,
  "remotes": 0,
  "in_msgs": 0,
  "out_msgs": 0,
  "in_bytes": 0,
  "out_bytes": 0,
  "slow_consumers": 0,
  "subscriptions": 0,
  "http_req_stats": {
    "/": 1,
    "/connz": 0,
    "/routez": 0,
    "/subsz": 0,
    "/varz": 1
  }
}
```

Clustering will be covered in more detail in the next chapter, but for now just remember that it can be configured with the --cluster flag. In Listing 4-7, you can see some of the options that can be set for clustering in the command line, although it is more convenient to configure these via the configuration file.

Listing 4-7. Clustering Options from the Server

```
Cluster Options:
        --routes <rurl-1, rurl-2>      Routes to solicit and
                                       connect
        --cluster <cluster-url>        Cluster URL for solicited
                                       routes
        --no_advertise <bool>          Advertise known cluster
                                       IPs to clients
        --connect_retries <number>     For implicit routes,
                                       number of connect retries
```

We must pass the full URI with the scheme in order to configure the listening port from the process (see Listing 4-8).

Listing 4-8. Setting the Clustering Port from the Server

```
$ gnatsd -m 8222 --cluster nats://127.0.0.1:6222

[43397] 2018/01/21 21:27:38.505490 [INF] Starting nats-server
version 1.0.4
[43397] 2018/01/21 21:27:38.505770 [INF] Starting http monitor
on 0.0.0.0:8222
[43397] 2018/01/21 21:27:38.505828 [INF] Listening for client
connections on 0.0.0.0:4222
[43397] 2018/01/21 21:27:38.505835 [INF] Server is ready
[43397] 2018/01/21 21:27:38.506120 [INF] Listening for route
connections on 127.0.0.1:6222
```

Note that the clients and clustering ports can be bound to different IP addresses. Listing 4-9 shows that it is possible to use one network interface for the traffic from the clients (--addr) and a different one for the internal traffic for clustering (--cluster).

Listing 4-9. Customizing clustering and bind from server

```
gnatsd --addr 10.0.1.1 --cluster nats://192.168.1.1:6222
```

We can also set the address the server should be binding to in the configuration file via the `listen` configuration option, although the address bound to the client part dictates which IP address the monitoring is going to be using if it's activated. In Listing 4-10, the server will bind to the `10.0.1.1` IP address so that clients are able to connect, but internally the cluster will be using a different IP address.

Listing 4-10. Binding Clients and Clustering to Different Interfaces

```
listen = 10.0.1.1:4222

http_port = 8222

cluster {
  listen = 192.168.1.1:6222
}
```

We will be taking a further look at how to configure clustering in the next chapter and learn more about monitoring in another chapter.

There is also another port that the server could potentially be exposed to by enabling the `-profiler` options for the server, as shown in Listing 4-11.

Listing 4-11. Setting a Profiling Port from the Server

```
$ gnatsd --logtime=false --profile 9090 &

[43927] [INF] Starting nats-server version 1.0.4
[43927] [INF] profiling port: 9090
[43927] [INF] Listening for client connections on 0.0.0.0:4222
[43927] [INF] Server is ready
```

```
$ go tool pprof http://127.0.0.1:9090/debug/pprof/goroutine
Fetching profile over HTTP from http://127.0.0.1:9090/debug/
pprof/goroutine
Saved profile in /Users/wallyqs/pprof/pprof.goroutine.002.pb.gz
Type: goroutine
Time: Jan 21, 2018 at 9:42pm (PST)
Entering interactive mode (type "help" for commands, "o" for
options)
(pprof) top
Showing nodes accounting for 9, 100% of 9 total
...
```

Note that this intended to be mostly for development and is not recommended for a production setting (other than to possibly help a root cause investigation if needed), so it is disabled by default. You can find more about how to use the profiler port to gather internal runtime statistics from the server by checking the usage guide from the pprof tool in the Go documentation at https://golang.org/pkg/runtime/pprof/.

Table 4-1 lists all the ports covered in this section.

Table 4-1. *Default Ports Used by NATS and Configuration Opts*

Ports	NATS Server	Docker	CLI Option	Config File
Clients	4222	4222	-p, -port PORT	listen: 0.0.0.0:PORT
Clustering	-	6222	-cluster nats://0.0.0.0:PORT	cluster { listen: 0.0.0.0:PORT}
Monitoring	-	8222	-m, -http_port PORT	http_port: PORT
Profiling	-	-	-profile	prof_port: PORT

Server Logging

The server will be silent by default, and most of the errors reported in the logs will be related to error cases (see Listing 4-12).

Listing 4-12. Logging Options from the Server

```
Logging Options:
    -l, --log <file>            File to redirect log output
    -T, --logtime               Timestamp log entries
                                (default: true)
    -s, --syslog                Log to syslog or windows
                                event log
    -r, --remote_syslog <addr>  Syslog server addr (udp://
                                localhost:514)
    -D, --debug                 Enable debugging output
    -V, --trace                 Trace the raw protocol
    -DV
```

For example, if someone accidentally makes an HTTP request to the client port instead of the monitoring port, this will be reported in the server logs as a parsing error. An example of this is found in Listing 4-13.

Listing 4-13. Using the Wrong Client to Connect to NATS

```
[26934] [INF] Starting nats-server version 1.0.4
[26934] [INF] Listening for client connections on 0.0.0.0:4222
[26934] [INF] Server is ready
[26934] [ERR] 127.0.0.1:63941 - cid:1 - Error reading from
client: Client Parser ERROR, state=0, i=0: proto='"GET /
HTTP/1.1\r\nHost: 127.0.0.1:"...'
```

The verbosity of the server logs can be changed by using the flags -D and -V, which are the debug and trace options respectively, in the configuration file. See Listing 4-14.

Listing 4-14. Activating Debugging and Tracing in the Configuration

```
listen = 0.0.0.0:4222
debug = true
trace = true
```

By using the -D and -V flags, we can elevate the logging level of the server. It should be noted that there is a significant performance hit for doing this, so it's only recommended when you're debugging and should not be used in production.

These flags can also be combined for convenience (-DV). Using both flags, we now get a bit more output, with the server logging the version of Go and an autogenerated server ID to identify the server. See Listing 4-15.

Listing 4-15. Combining Debugging and Tracing Using the –DV Flag

```
$ gnatsd -DV
[46498] 2018/01/21 21:59:05.214042 [INF] Starting nats-server
version 1.0.4
[46498] 2018/01/21 21:59:05.214252 [DBG] Go build version
go1.9.2
[46498] 2018/01/21 21:59:05.214591 [INF] Listening for client
connections on 0.0.0.0:4222
[46498] 2018/01/21 21:59:05.214610 [DBG] Server id is
ubUB792DgUNtQ3nQ6JYcg1
[46498] 2018/01/21 21:59:05.214616 [INF] Server is ready
[46498] 2018/01/21 22:09:21.805622 [DBG] 127.0.0.1:49364 -
cid:1 - Client connection created
```

Now, whenever a client connects to the server, it will appear in the server logs, as shown in Listing 4-16.

Listing 4-16. Combining Debugging and Tracing Using the –DV
Flag

```
$ gnatsd -DV
...
[46498] 2018/01/21 22:09:21.805622 [DBG] 127.0.0.1:49364 -
cid:1 - Client connection created
```

When a message is published or forwarded by the server, it will be
logged as well, as shown in Listing 4-17.

Listing 4-17. Tracing Output from the Server

```
$ gnatsd -DV
[46543] 2018/01/21 22:09:21.805622 [DBG] 127.0.0.1:49364 -
cid:1 - Client connection created
[46543] 2018/01/21 22:11:21.815683 [DBG] 127.0.0.1:49364 -
cid:1 - Client Ping Timer
[46543] 2018/01/21 22:11:21.815817 [TRC] 127.0.0.1:49364 -
cid:1 - <<- [PING]
[46543] 2018/01/21 22:11:33.501252 [TRC] 127.0.0.1:49364 -
cid:1 -->> [SUB hello 90]
[46543] 2018/01/21 22:11:33.501319 [TRC] 127.0.0.1:49364 -
cid:1 - <<- [OK]
[46543] 2018/01/21 22:11:35.193158 [TRC] 127.0.0.1:49364 -
cid:1 -->> [PUB hello 5]
[46543] 2018/01/21 22:11:35.821924 [TRC] 127.0.0.1:49364 -
cid:1 -->> MSG_PAYLOAD: [world]
[46543] 2018/01/21 22:11:35.821954 [TRC] 127.0.0.1:49364 -
cid:1 - <<- [OK]
[46543] 2018/01/21 22:11:35.821985 [TRC] 127.0.0.1:49364 -
cid:1 - <<- [MSG hello 90 5]
```

The logging time can be deactivated in the client by setting `logtime` to false, as shown in Listing 4-18.

Listing 4-18. Disabling Log Time from the Server

```
$ gnatsd --logtime=false -DV
[46452] [INF] Starting nats-server version 1.0.4
[46452] [DBG] Go build version go1.9.2
[46452] [INF] Listening for client connections on 0.0.0.0:4222
[46452] [DBG] Server id is fL74Kpq6HQcVXesLpnTeyb
[46452] [INF] Server is ready
```

Logging Outputs

The server logs its output to `stderr` by default, but it is also possible to configure a file or syslog as the logging output. To use a file to log the output, the `--log` flag can be specified with a path to the logging file (shown in Listing 4-19).

Listing 4-19. Logging into an Output File

```
$ gnatsd --log /var/log/nats.log
```

For syslog support, both local and remote syslog is supported. We can log locally into syslog, as shown in Listing 4-20.

Listing 4-20. Logging into an Output File via syslog

```
$ gnatsd --syslog

$ tail -f /var/log/system.log

Jan 21 22:26:34 gnatsd[46864]: Listening for client connections
on 0.0.0.0:4222
Jan 21 22:26:34 gnatsd[46864]: Server is ready
```

```
Jan 21 22:26:37 gnatsd[46864]: 127.0.0.1:49425 - cid:1 -->>
[PUB hello 5]
Jan 21 22:26:38 gnatsd[46864]: 127.0.0.1:49425 - cid:1 -->>
MSG_PAYLOAD: [world]
...
```

These features are there for completeness and can be useful, but it is a more recommended practice to delegate this task to another system. For example, if daemonized, then something like systemd ought to be managing persisting the logs onto a file, and if we are running NATS in a container orchestration system such as Kubernetes or Cloud Foundry, the best practice is to log to stdout/stderr (see https://12factor.net/logs) and delegate to the platform how to handle logging.

Configuring Authorization

Using the command line, it is possible to set a general pair of credentials for users to connect to the server, or to use an auth token (see Listing 4-21 and Listing 4-22).

Listing 4-21. Auth Options

```
Authorization Options:
        --user <user>        User required for connections
        --pass <password>    Password required for connections
        --auth <token>       Authorization token required for
                             connections
```

Listing 4-22. Auth Options from the Command Line

```
$ gnatsd -user fuga -pass hoge
```

Now when the client tries to publish a message before specifying the credentials, it will be disconnected by the server with an error (see Listing 4-23).

Listing 4-23. Resulting Error from the Server Protocol

```
$ telnet 127.0.0.1 4222
INFO {"server_id":"qEWnRxHCP4ipPzQo1WYCRY",...,
"max_payload":1048576}
pub hello 5
-ERR 'Authorization Violation'
```

The credentials can also be set in the configuration file by using the authorization stanza (see Listing 4-24).

Listing 4-24. Setting Authorization Credentials using a configuration file

```
listen = 0.0.0.0:4222

authorization {
  username = hoge
  password = fuga
}
```

Once the credentials are set, a client can use the CONNECT command with a payload containing the credentials in order to establish a connection (see Listing 4-25).

Listing 4-25. Establishing a Connection

```
$ gnatsd --config code/client-auth.conf &

$ telnet 127.0.0.1 4222
INFO {"server_id":"UWlg2Qa36XdhNx9wY7eOtS",...,
"max_payload":1048576}
```

```
CONNECT {"user":"hoge","pass":"fuga"}
+OK
pub hello 5
world
+OK
```

You can find out how to set the authentication credentials by reading the NATS clients section in Chapter 3.

Extending the Authorization Deadline

If a client fails to send a CONNECT protocol with a payload containing the correct authentication credentials before the authorization timeout (which is two seconds by default), it will be disconnected (see Listing 4-26).

Listing 4-26. Setting Authorization Credentials via the command line

```
$ gnatsd -user hoge -pass fuga
[50383] 2018/01/22 00:31:50.762676 [INF] Starting nats-server
version 1.0.4
[50383] 2018/01/22 00:31:50.762976 [INF] Listening for client
connections on 0.0.0.0:4222
[50383] 2018/01/22 00:31:50.762986 [INF] Server is ready

$ telnet 127.0.0.1 4222
INFO {"server_id":"m25WKFnqy1LtQvdOsEZJnV",...,"max_
payload":1048576}
-ERR 'Authorization Timeout'
```

There might be cases when network latency induces a client to time out when connecting. In those cases, the authorization deadline can be extended via the configuration file, as shown in Listing 4-27.

Listing 4-27. Extending the Authorization Timeout Deadline

```
listen = 0.0.0.0:4222

authorization {
  username = hoge
  password = fuga
  timeout = 5
}
```

TLS Options

We learn in more detail how to secure a NATS installation and how to use TLS in a later chapter. Like with the clustering settings, TLS can be set via the command line (see Listing 4-28), but it's more convenient to configure it via the config file.

Listing 4-28. TLS Configuration Options

```
TLS Options:
        --tls                   Enable TLS, do not verify
                                clients (default: false)
        --tlscert <file>        Server certificate file
        --tlskey <file>         Private key for server
                                certificate
        --tlsverify             Enable TLS, verify client
                                certificates
        --tlscacert <file>      Client certificate CA for
                                verification
```

Tuning the Defaults

Out of the box, the server has good defaults that work for most general cases, although sometimes we'll need to tune them in order to accommodate our use case. In this section, you find a list of these advanced settings, which can only be configured via the configuration file.

Increasing the Maximum Payload Size

Since the start of the NATS project, a single MB has been kept as the maximum payload size that a client can send at once. Ideally, this setting should be kept as is with the use of a chunking strategy client-side (or another type of plumbing for larger blobs of data), but the server does allow us to extend this payload and it still works pretty well.

Listing 4-29 shows an example of increasing the limit from the server to 5MB.

Listing 4-29. The Max Payload Configuration Option

```
listen = 0.0.0.0:4444
max_payload = 5242880
```

Now in the INFO message on connect, the server will announce the higher limit. Sending messages less than that limit will not result in -ERR 'Maximum Payload Violation' protocol errors (see Listing 4-30).

Listing 4-30. The Max Payload Configuration Option Can Be Extended

```
$ gnatsd -c code/maximum-payload.conf
[48380] 2018/01/21 23:34:19.302493 [INF] Starting nats-server
version 1.0.4
```

```
[48380] 2018/01/21 23:34:19.303170 [INF] Listening for client
connections on 0.0.0.0:4444
[48380] 2018/01/21 23:34:19.303186 [INF] Server is ready

$ telnet 127.0.0.1 4444
INFO {"server_id":"0BJ5V5mbTrGjOB1Df9HTN7",...,
"max_payload":5242880}
pub hello 1048579
...
```

Extending the Deadline for Slow Consumers Handling

By default, a client is considered to be a slow consumer when the server has to send messages to it but the client is not draining them from the socket in the two-second deadline.

This setting can be tuned by modifying write_deadline in the server, using a time duration string. Listing 4-31 shows how to extend it to detect a slow consumer that takes more than five seconds.

Listing 4-31. Extending the Slow Consumer Deadline

```
listen = 0.0.0.0:4444

write_deadline = "5s
```

This can affect performance in the server overall when there are slow consumers in the system. The server will not start sending bytes to the next client until it is done sending to the slow consumer, thus slow customers can increase the overall tail latencies in the credentials.

Tuning the Keepalive Interval

Sometimes, we may want to change how aggressive the keepalive
PING/PONG interval is when detecting unhealthy clients. There are two
options in the configuration file that can help with this—ping_max for
tuning how many PONG replies can be missed and ping_interval, which
dictates how often the server will be health checking (see Listing 4-32).

Listing 4-32. Customizing the Keepalive Interval

```
listen = 0.0.0.0:4444

# Disconnect after the 3rd PONG reply is missed
ping_max = 3

# Ping every 30s
ping_interval = 30
```

Tuning the Maximum Number of Connections

The maximum number of connections by default in the server is 65,536,
but it can be decreased to limit the number of connections that we may
want to have in the server at once. For the purposes of an example, let's
limit this to a single connection (see Listing 4-33).

Listing 4-33. Setting the Max Connections to One

```
listen = 0.0.0.0:4444

# Limit to a single connection,
max_connections = 1
```

Now, when the second connection is being made, it will fail with a
protocol error, as shown in Listing 4-34.

Listing 4-34. Failing with a Protocol Error

```
$ telnet 127.0.0.1 4222
INFO {"server_id":"opUbltMuhTu18Mdv6ywoW8",...,
"max_payload":1048576}
-ERR 'Maximum Connections Exceeded'
```

Server Reloading

Starting from the v1.0.0 release from the server, it now supports for on-the-fly reconfiguration by sending a HUP signal to the server process when using a configuration file.

Reloading to Activate Tracing On-the-Fly

For example, we can start the server without verbose logging enabled in the configuration file, as shown in Listing 4-35, and then start it (see Listing 4-36).

Listing 4-35. Customizing Debug and Trace Logging Levels using a Config File

```
listen = 0.0.0.0:4222

debug = false
trace = false
```

Listing 4-36. Starting server using config file that can be reloaded

```
$ gnatsd -c code/reload-trace.conf  &
[50792] [INF] Listening for client connections on 0.0.0.0:4222
[50792] [INF] Server is ready
...
```

Then, the file is modified to activate tracing with a new configuration, as shown Listing 4-37.

Listing 4-37. Enabling Debug and Trace options in Config File

```
listen = 0.0.0.0:4222

debug = true # false
trace = true # false
```

After sending the HUP signal to the process, the new connections in the cluster will have their messages traced (see Listing 4-38).

Listing 4-38. Reloading the Logging Options via HUP signal

```
...
[50792] 2018/01/22 00:38:24.098814 [INF] Reloaded: trace = true
[50792] 2018/01/22 00:38:24.098848 [INF] Reloaded: debug = true
[50792] 2018/01/22 00:38:24.098879 [INF] Reloaded server
configuration

$ telnet 127.0.0.1 4222
pub hello 5
world
+OK

...
[50792] [DBG] 127.0.0.1:50279 - cid:1 - Client Ping Timer
[50792] [DBG] 127.0.0.1:50285 - cid:4 - Client connection
created
[50792] [TRC] 127.0.0.1:50285 - cid:4 -->> [PUB hello 5]
[50792] [TRC] 127.0.0.1:50285 - cid:4 -->> MSG_PAYLOAD: [world]
[50792] [TRC] 127.0.0.1:50285 - cid:4 - <<- [OK]
```

Reducing the Number of Live Connections

The number of maximum connections can be changed on demand as well by sending a HUP signal to the process. One consequence of this is that if clients are already connected to the system, a number of them will have their connection reset.

In another aggressive example, let's say that we limited the number of clients to be 10 and then change it to 1 (see Listing 4-39 and Listing 4-40).

Listing 4-39. Configuring Max Number of Connections using a Config File

```
listen = 0.0.0.0:4222

max_connections = 10
```

Listing 4-40. Decreasing Max Connections to a single one before reloading

```
listen = 0.0.0.0:4222

max_connections = 1 # 10
```

Now when sending HUP, it will pick up the changes and *randomly* disconnect some of the clients in order to have as many as the max_connections option dictates (see Listing 4-41).

Listing 4-41. Reloading Max Connections via HUP signal

```
$ sudo kill -HUP 50994

$ gnatsd -c code/max-conns-1.conf
[50994] [INF] Starting nats-server version 1.0.4
[50994] [INF] Listening for client connections on 0.0.0.0:4222
[50994] [INF] Server is ready
[50994] [ERR] 127.0.0.1:50303 - cid:1 - Maximum Connections
Exceeded
```

```
[50994] [ERR] 127.0.0.1:50304 - cid:2 - Maximum Connections
Exceeded
[50994] [INF] Closed 2 connections to fall within max_
connections
[50994] [INF] Reloaded: max_connections = 1
[50994] [INF] Reloaded server configuration
```

Running NATS in Docker

The NATS team maintains an official Docker image, which makes it easier
to deploy on container orchestration systems as well as different OS
architectures (container images for Windows and ARM are also available).
Unlike bare gnatsd, the official Docker image binds by default all the
common ports from the server, so it is only left to expose them via the
Docker tool (v17.12.0-ce as of this writing) Listing 4-42 shows this process.

Listing 4-42. Running NATS in Docker

```
$ docker run -p 4222:4222 -p 8222:8222 -p 6222:6222 nats
[1] 2018/01/19 21:43:49.034896 [INF] Starting nats-server
version 1.0.4
[1] 2018/01/19 21:43:49.035076 [INF] Starting http monitor on
0.0.0.0:8222
[1] 2018/01/19 21:43:49.035121 [INF] Listening for client
connections on 0.0.0.0:4222
[1] 2018/01/19 21:43:49.035125 [INF] Server is ready
[1] 2018/01/19 21:43:49.035314 [INF] Listening for route
connections on 0.0.0.0:6222
```

The -P option in Docker exposes all the ports and maps them to a random port, so that could be done as well for convenience. In the snippet in Listing 4-43, -d is used to detach the container and run it in the background.

Listing 4-43. Detaching the Container and Running It in the Background

```
$ docker run -P -d nats
e626b0323dc033e5b78994c00e3120e86e659c44b1687da00e0bc46f5648239f

$ docker port e626b0323dc033e5b78994
4222/tcp -> 0.0.0.0:32792
6222/tcp -> 0.0.0.0:32791
8222/tcp -> 0.0.0.0:32790

$ docker logs e626b0323dc033e5b78994
```

As you can see, the gnatsd binary becomes the PID 1 within the container. The official NATS Docker image is built using a FROM scratch container with a multistep build process, which makes it a very lightweight image and fast to pull. However, it is not possible to use sh/bash based custom health checks in the container as some container orchestration systems require.

Summary

In this chapter, we went through some of the most relevant parts to consider when configuring a NATS Server. You need to keep these in mind when preparing to set up NATS in your production environment.

Keep in mind that the most up-to-date guide on how to configure the NATS Server can always be found in the README from the gnatsd repository (https://github.com/nats-io/gnatsd/blob/master/README.md).

CHAPTER 5

High Availability with NATS Clustering

NATS features a clustering mode that helps improve the reliability of the service by making it more tolerant to server failures. If the server that a client is connected to fails for some reason or goes away, a cluster-aware NATS client can then reconnect to any other available server in the cluster.

In this chapter, we take a look at few examples of how to set up a cluster in different scenarios and share considerations on how to make the best use of the clustering mode from NATS.

The NATS Cluster Network Topology

A group of NATS Servers form a cluster by having them all connected to each other. It is a full-mesh one-hop network setup, so a client can be connected to any of the nodes in the cluster. The server to which they are connected will then be responsible of forwarding the message to the other nodes in the cluster according to the interest graph. Figure 5-1 shows a sample topology of a NATS cluster setup consisting of three nodes and a pair of clients communicating and sending messages on a hello subject without both clients being connected to the same NATS Server.

© Waldemar Quevedo 2018
W. Quevedo, *Practical NATS*, https://doi.org/10.1007/978-1-4842-3570-6_5

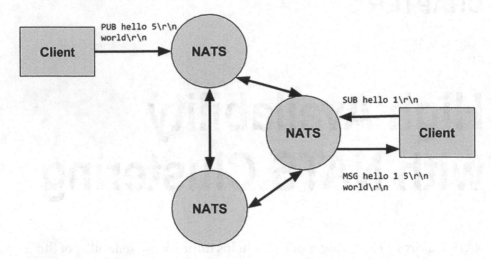

Figure 5-1. *A three-node NATS cluster*

Upon server failure, the available NATS clients will by default reconnect to one of the other serves in the pool *randomly*. In Figure 5-2, one of the NATS servers has failed, so the client that was connected to it has failed over to another one of the servers that is available in the pool.

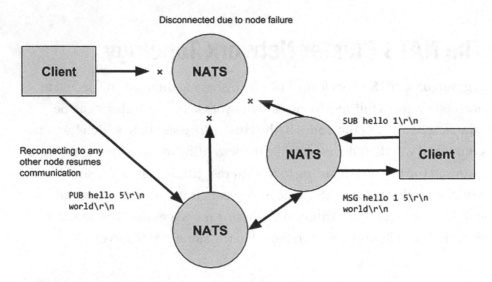

Figure 5-2. *Recovering from a server failure*

The clustering mode can greatly help NATS servers sharing the load, as a message will only hop from one server to another following the interest graph.

Something to keep in mind though is that it is a full-mesh topology, which means the more servers there are in the cluster, the larger the number of connections and amount of traffic that goes through the network. Because of the full-mesh topology, a 10-node cluster requires 45 extra TCP connections between the nodes for the sole purpose of routing the messages to the clients and a 14-node cluster needs almost a hundred (see Figure 5-3). For this reason, it is recommended for cluster sizes to be on the small side, with around three to five nodes as part of a cluster.

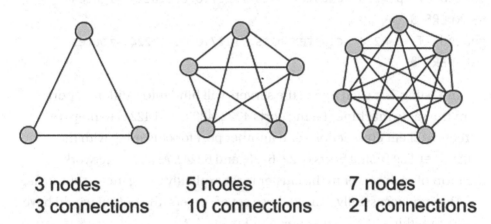

3 nodes
3 connections

5 nodes
10 connections

7 nodes
21 connections

Figure 5-3. *Example NATS cluster topologies*

Configuring a NATS Cluster from the CLI

A simple three-node cluster can be set up from the command line, as shown in Listing 5-1.

Listing 5-1. Cluster Formation via the Command Line

```
SERVERS=nats://127.0.0.1:6222,nats://127.0.0.1:6223,na
ts://127.0.0.1:6224

gnatsd -T -p 4222 -cluster nats://127.0.0.1:6222 -routes
$SERVERS &
gnatsd -T -p 4223 -cluster nats://127.0.0.1:6223 -routes
$SERVERS &
gnatsd -T -p 4224 -cluster nats://127.0.0.1:6224 -routes
$SERVERS &
```

In Listing 5-1, each one of the servers will bind into a different port from the same machine (taking ports 4222, 4223, and 4224) to prepare to receive client connections and another port for clustering with the --cluster flag (using ports 6222, 6223, and 6224). Also, the network location of each server in the cluster is set explicitly using the --routes flag.

Having successfully started these set of servers, the output would have been something like what's shown in Listing 5-2.

Listing 5-2. Cluster Formation Logs

```
# Server #1 starts (pid=52263)
[52263] [INF] Starting nats-server version 1.0.4
[52263] [INF] Listening for client connections on 0.0.0.0:4222
[52263] [INF] Server is ready
[52263] [INF] Listening for route connections on 127.0.0.1:6222
```

114

```
[52263] [INF] 127.0.0.1:51019 - rid:1 - Route connection
created
[52263] [INF] 127.0.0.1:6222 - rid:2 - Route connection created

# Server #2 joins (pid=52268)
[52268] [INF] Listening for client connections on 0.0.0.0:4223
[52268] [INF] Server is ready
[52268] [INF] Listening for route connections on 127.0.0.1:6223
[52268] [INF] 127.0.0.1:51024 - rid:3 - Route connection
created
[52263] [INF] 127.0.0.1:51023 - rid:3 - Route connection
created
[52268] [INF] 127.0.0.1:6222 - rid:1 - Route connection created
[52268] [INF] 127.0.0.1:6223 - rid:2 - Route connection created
[52268] [INF] 127.0.0.1:51025 - rid:4 - Route connection
created
[52263] [INF] 127.0.0.1:6223 - rid:4 - Route connection created

# Server #3 joins too (52273)
[52273] [INF] Listening for client connections on 0.0.0.0:4224
[52273] [INF] Server is ready
[52273] [INF] Listening for route connections on 127.0.0.1:6224
[52273] [INF] 127.0.0.1:51037 - rid:4 - Route connection
created
[52273] [INF] 127.0.0.1:6223 - rid:3 - Route connection created
[52273] [INF] 127.0.0.1:6224 - rid:1 - Route connection created
[52273] [INF] 127.0.0.1:6222 - rid:2 - Route connection created
[52263] [INF] 127.0.0.1:51038 - rid:5 - Route connection
created
[52268] [INF] 127.0.0.1:51039 - rid:5 - Route connection
created
[52263] [INF] 127.0.0.1:6224 - rid:6 - Route connection created
```

```
[52273] [INF] 127.0.0.1:51040 - rid:5 - Route connection
created
[52273] [INF] 127.0.0.1:51041 - rid:6 - Route connection
created

# Cluster fully assembled now
[52268] [INF] 127.0.0.1:6224 - rid:6 - Route connection created
```

Listing 5-3 shows that when connecting to the first node in the cluster via telnet, we can find that there is now an extra connect_urls field in the initial INFO message.

Listing 5-3. Cluster Formation via the Command Line

```
$ telnet 127.0.0.1 4222
Trying 127.0.0.1...
Connected to localhost.
Escape character is '^]'.
INFO {...,"connect_urls":["192.168.1.9:4223","192.168.1.9:4224"
]}
```

This field is indicating to the client that there are two other servers in the cluster that are available to connect in case there would be a failure with the current server. Let's leave that telnet client connected and also make a wildcard subscription to receive all the messages in the cluster (see Listing 5-4)

Listing 5-4. Subscribing with Full Wildcard to Cluster

```
$ telnet 127.0.0.1 4222
...
SUB > 1
+OK
```

Next, let's connect to server 3 in the cluster using the Go client (see Listing 5-5).

Listing 5-5. Connecting to a NATS Cluster

```
package main

import (
        "log"
        "runtime"

        "github.com/nats-io/go-nats"
)
func main() {
        nc, err := nats.Connect("nats://127.0.0.1:4224")
        if err != nil {
                log.Fatalf("Error: %s", err)
        }
        log.Println("All Servers:", nc.Servers())
        log.Println("Discovered Servers:",
        nc.DiscoveredServers())

        nc.Subscribe("hi", func(m *nats.Msg) {
                log.Println("[Received] ", string(m.Data))
        })

        nc.Publish("hi", []byte("hello world"))

        runtime.Goexit()
}
```

Even though we only configured a single endpoint, we can see that the client is aware that there is another extra pair of servers to which it can connect. This new pair of servers were picked up *implicitly* from the initial

INFO message when the client connected to the server. Modern NATS clients have this capability. In Listing 5-6, we can see that the client is now aware of the other accessible endpoints in the cluster.

Listing 5-6. Client Aware of Other Servers in the Cluster

```
$ go run code/implicit-servers.go
2018/01/22 04:00:03 Available Servers: [nats://127.0.0.1:4224
nats://192.168.1.9:4223 nats://192.168.1.9:4222]
2018/01/22 04:00:03 Discovered Servers:
[nats://192.168.1.9:4223 nats://192.168.1.9:4222]
```

Then in the telnet session that was started at Listing 5-4, a single hello world message would have been received, even though the clients are not connected to the same NATS server. Listing 5-7 shows how how the telnet client received a message on the hi subject.

Listing 5-7. Cluster Formation via the Command Line

```
$ telnet 127.0.0.1 4222
Trying 127.0.0.1...
Connected to localhost.
Escape character is '^]'.
INFO {...,"connect_urls":["192.168.1.9:4223","192.168.1.9:4224"
]}
sub > 1
+OK
MSG hi 1 11
hello world
```

Next, let's kill the server to which the Go client is connected (see Listing 5-8).

Listing 5-8. Killing a Server in the Cluster

```
kill -TERM 52273
```

This would have triggered the reconnection logic from the Go client, and then it will failover to another server. If a message is published by the telnet session, it will still be received since the client has already reconnected to another node in the cluster (see Listing 5-9).

Listing 5-9. Killing a Server in the Cluster

```
$ telnet 127.0.0.1 4224
PUB hi 12
hello world!
+OK

# Go Client
2018/01/22 04:16:16 [Received]  hello world!
```

By default, the NATS Server uses this autodiscovery feature to locate new servers in the cluster. For cloud-native scenarios, this is very handy, since we might not know all the network addresses from the nodes beforehand, so it would be more convenient to gradually increase the size of the cluster by having nodes join the cluster.

Setting Up Clustering via the Configuration File

One of the things that was left pending in the previous chapter is to cover more in-depth how to configure clusters using the configuration file. In Listings 5-10, 5-11, and 5-12 show a sample configuration of a three-node cluster using the cluster stanza from the configuration file. We split these into three different files since we need one per server in this case.

Listing 5-10. Configuring to a Three-Node NATS Cluster (Server 1)

```
# server-1.conf
listen = 0.0.0.0:4222

cluster {
  listen = 0.0.0.0:6222

  routes = [
    nats://127.0.0.1:6223
    nats://127.0.0.1:6224
  ]
}
```

Listing 5-11. Configuring to a Three-Node NATS Cluster (Server 2)

```
# server-2.conf
listen = 0.0.0.0:4223

cluster {
  listen = 0.0.0.0:6223

  routes = [
    nats://127.0.0.1:6222
    nats://127.0.0.1:6224
  ]
}
```

Listing 5-12. Configuring to a Three-Node NATS Cluster (Server 3)

```
# server-3.conf
listen = 0.0.0.0:4224

cluster {
  listen = 0.0.0.0:6224
```

```
routes = [
  nats://127.0.0.1:6222
  nats://127.0.0.1:6223
]
}
```

In the routes section, we are defining that there are three nodes in the cluster *explicitly*.

Explicitly Setting a Server Pool in the Client

In the Go client, we can do the same and set all the nodes in the cluster explicitly rather than via autodiscovery, by passing a comma-separated list of servers (see Listing 5-13).

Listing 5-13. Setting the Explicit List of a Three-Node NATS Cluster

```
package main

import (
        "log"
        "runtime"

        "github.com/nats-io/go-nats"
)

func main() {
        servers := "nats://127.0.0.1:4222,nats://127.0.0.1:
        4223,nats://127.0.0.1:4224"
        nc, err := nats.Connect(servers)
        if err != nil {
                log.Fatalf("Error: %s", err)
        }
```

```
        log.Println("All Servers:", nc.Servers())
        log.Println("Discovered Servers:",
        nc.DiscoveredServers())

        nc.Subscribe("hi", func(m *nats.Msg) {
                log.Println("[Received] ", string(m.Data))
        })

        nc.Publish("hi", []byte("hello world"))

        runtime.Goexit()
}
```

Disabling Random Reconnection Ordering

By default, the Go client will be connecting to one of the nodes randomly, but this can be disabled so that the reconnect attempts are tried in order. We do this by passing the DontRandomize option (see Listing 5-14). Most available NATS clients implement this helper logic.

Listing 5-14. Keep Ordering for Reconnection in Server Pool

```
package main

import (
        "log"
        "runtime"

        "github.com/nats-io/go-nats"
)

func main() {
        servers := "nats://127.0.0.1:4222,nats://127.0.0.1:4223
        ,nats://127.0.0.1:4224"
        nc, err := nats.Connect(servers, nats.DontRandomize())
```

```
if err != nil {
        log.Fatalf("Error: %s", err)
}
log.Println("All Servers:", nc.Servers())
log.Println("Discovered Servers:",
nc.DiscoveredServers())

nc.Subscribe("hi", func(m *nats.Msg) {
        log.Println("[Received] ", string(m.Data))
})

nc.Publish("hi", []byte("hello world"))

runtime.Goexit()
}
```

Bootstrapping a Cluster Using Autodiscovery

In the previous sections, the cluster has been assembled by setting the list of nodes explicitly, but it's also possible to do this using autodiscovery to join the cluster and share the routes to other nodes. Listing 5-15 shows an example of a three-node cluster, where they all connect to the first server, which was started to become a cluster.

Listing 5-15. Using Autodiscovery to Bootstrap a Cluster

```
gnatsd -T -p 4222 -cluster nats://127.0.0.1:6222 -routes
nats://127.0.0.1:6222 &
gnatsd -T -p 4223 -cluster nats://127.0.0.1:6223 -routes
nats://127.0.0.1:6222 &
gnatsd -T -p 4224 -cluster nats://127.0.0.1:6224 -routes
nats://127.0.0.1:6222 &
```

Establishing a telnet session, we can see the same result as earlier (see Listing 5-16). We can perceive the different `connect_urls` from the nodes in the cluster.

Listing 5-16. Server Autodiscovery via the INFO Protocol

```
$ telnet 127.0.0.1 4223
Trying 127.0.0.1...
Connected to localhost.
Escape character is '^]'.
INFO {...,"connect_urls":["192.168.1.9:4222","192.168.1.9:4224"
]}
```

In this case, the first server exposing the 6222 port is becoming a *seed node* and the other servers in the cluster will discover the servers by relying on the seed server. If the seed server node fails, the clients will reconnect to one of the remaining nodes in the cluster. One limitation from this though is that if there is a new server that wants to join and the seed server is unavailable, it will fail to join until the seed server is back again.

Monitoring a NATS Cluster State

When exposing the monitoring port from the server, it is possible to inspect the state of the cluster from the perspective of one of the nodes by making a GET request to `/routez` (see Listing 5-17). This can be useful for running a quickly check to determine whether the cluster has been fully assembled and to debug the configuration further.

Listing 5-17. Routez Data from a Three-Node Cluster

```
curl http://127.0.0.1:8222/routez
{
  "now": "2018-01-21T17:47:24.626807-08:00",
  "num_routes": 2,
```

```
   "routes": [
     {
       "rid": 3,
       "remote_id": "whf2vBGtE1Blm7a7eDbgOh",
       "did_solicit": false,
       "is_configured": false,
       "ip": "127.0.0.1",
       "port": 62223,
       "pending_size": 0,
       "in_msgs": 0,
       "out_msgs": 0,
       "in_bytes": 0,
       "out_bytes": 0,
       "subscriptions": 0
     },
     {
       "rid": 4,
       "remote_id": "ntQEo3fvVi7ptiB3EF8jpo",
       "did_solicit": falsc,
       "is_configured": false,
       "ip": "127.0.0.1",
       "port": 62226,
       "pending_size": 0,
       "in_msgs": 0,
       "out_msgs": 0,
       "in_bytes": 0,
       "out_bytes": 0,
       "subscriptions": 0
     }
   ]
}
```

On Autodiscovery and Load Balancers

The server autodiscovery mode might not be very helpful in certain types of deployments where there is no network connectivity between the client and the set of IP addresses that are announced to it.

This may happen, for example, when there is a TCP load balancer in the middle (see Figure 5-4). The client will attempt to connect to the NATS service by using the IP from the load balancer, and then in return, the IPs from the cluster will be announced to it. But if these are unreachable, there is no point in having them announced. When the server detaches or fails, the client will futilely attempt to connect to those IPs, thus increasing the time to recover.

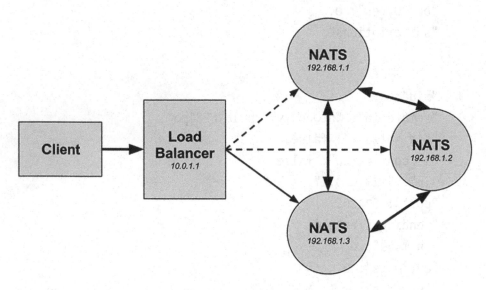

Figure 5-4. NATS Server cluster behind a load balancer

In order to disable this, there is the no_advertise option, which will make the server avoid announcing the connect_urls field in the INFO messages to the clients.

Listing 5-18. Disabling Advertising of Endpoints in Cluster

```
$ gnatsd --no_advertise
```

Setting Up a NATS Cluster Behind a Load Balancer

In Listing 5-19, you can find a minimal HAProxy configuration that sets a round-robin load balancing policy among a three-node cluster. Clients will be connecting to the HAProxy process that is binding to 10.0.1.1:4222, and the HAProxy will be responsible for periodically ensuring that the servers in the pool are alive by making an HTTP request to the monitoring port from each of the nodes in the cluster (on port 8222).

Listing 5-19. Sample HAProxy NATS Setup

```
frontend nats_service
    bind 10.0.1.1:4222
    mode tcp
    default_backend nats_cluster_nodes

backend nats_cluster_nodes
    balance roundrobin

    # Custom health check done to the HTTP port
    option httpchk get /varz

    server node1 172.16.0.1:4222 check port 8222
    server node2 172.16.0.2:4222 check port 8222
    server node3 172.16.0.3:4222 check port 8222
```

We can assemble the three-node cluster explicitly by using the configuration shown in Listing 5-20 in all the server nodes. This configuration can be reused by all the nodes in the pool since NATS will just skip trying to connect to a route where it resides (by checking the server ID filed that was retrieved from the INFO connect).

Listing 5-20. Disabling Autodiscovery

```
listen = 0.0.0.0:4222

http_port = 8222

cluster {
 listen = 0.0.0.0:6222

 # Disables advertising 'connect_urls' to clients
 no_advertise = true

 routes = [
    nats://172.16.0.1:6222
    nats://172.16.0.2:6222
    nats://172.16.0.3:6222
 ]
}
```

Now let's start it with the autodiscovery disabled and try to connect to it (see Listing 5-21). We should notice that there is no connect_urls field anymore.

Listing 5-21. Starting gnatsd Without Advertising IPs

```
$ gnatsd -c code/disable-advertising.conf
[35544] [INF] Starting nats-server version 1.0.4
[35544] [INF] Starting http monitor on 0.0.0.0:8222
[35544] [INF] Listening for client connections on 0.0.0.0:4222
[35544] [INF] Server is ready

$ telnet 127.0.0.1 4222
INFO {"server_id":"3wEBoCq4Al1YttDlB2fIav",...,
"max_payload":1048576}
```

Then the clients just have to point to the IP from the load balancer and connect to it (see Listing 5-22).

Listing 5-22. Disabling Autodiscovery

```go
package main

import (
        "log"
        "runtime"

        "github.com/nats-io/go-nats"
)

func main() {
        nc, err := nats.Connect("nats://10.0.1.1:4222")
        if err != nil {
                log.Fatalf("Error: %s", err)
        }
        nc.Subscribe("greeting", func(m *nats.Msg) {
                log.Printf("[Received] %s", string(m.Data))
        })

        for i := 0; i < 10; i++ {
                nc.Publish("greeting", []byte("hello world!!!"))
        }
        nc.Flush()

        runtime.Goexit()
}
```

As demonstrated, it is possible to set up a NATS cluster behind a load balancer, *but* there is still one big limitation. If you're considering using TLS, it is currently not possible as documented in the issue 291 from the gnatsd repository (https://github.com/nats-io/gnatsd/issues/291). Clients in NATS have to first receive the INFO protocol in plain text before being signaled to upgrade into a TLS connection, so it is not possible to establish a TLS connection from the start. This may be resolved in a future release.

Summary

This chapter marks the end of the first half of this book. We are more than ready and with enough knowledge of the fundamentals and inner workings about NATS to be able to tackle developing a production-ready application that uses NATS for its control plane.

CHAPTER 6

Developing a Cloud-Native NATS Application

In this chapter, we put into practice what was covered in the first half of the book and develop an application that uses NATS for the discovery and makes requests of services that are parts of the system.

As an example, we implement a NATS Rider service that helps users request a driver on-demand in order to reach a destination. Externally users talk to the service by using HTTP, but internally all the communication flows through NATS.

The NATS Rider Application

The NATS Rider application follows a microservices architecture with the different parts of the system all decoupled from each other, establishing boundaries in terms of the responsibility that each should have.

© Waldemar Quevedo 2018
W. Quevedo, *Practical NATS*, https://doi.org/10.1007/978-1-4842-3570-6_6

The system is decomposed into three main components:

- The *API Server* exposes an HTTP endpoint to which users can make requests to find an available driver.

- A *Rides Manager* server component is responsible for finding available drivers.

- A *Driver Agent* is inside of the cars and is always connected to a NATS node in the cluster.

Figure 6-1 shows a sample flow of a request from a user to find a driver.

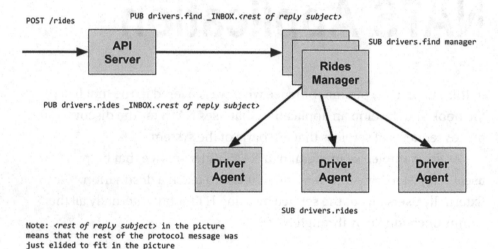

Figure 6-1. Example flow a request

Figure 6-2 shows a high-level view image of the application's architecture, including the NATS cluster that we will be using from the beginning.

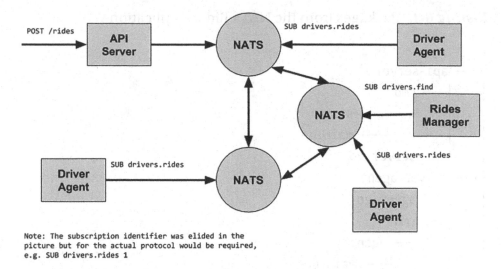

Figure 6-2. *NATS Rider application architecture overview*

Components connected to the NATS cluster can come and go and just need to be connected to any NATS Server that is part of the NATS cluster. The NATS clustering implementation will be responsible for routing the messages properly among the different nodes.

Scaffolding the Application

We will be using Go and the official Go NATS client for developing the application. Listing 6-1 shows the goal folder structure for the application containing the implementation of the three main components of the system.

Listing 6-1. Packages from the NATS Rider Application

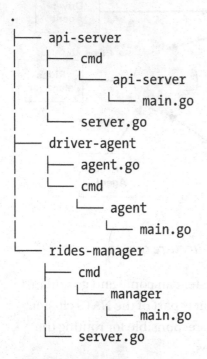

```
.
├── api-server
│   ├── cmd
│   │   └── api-server
│   │       └── main.go
│   └── server.go
├── driver-agent
│   ├── agent.go
│   └── cmd
│       └── agent
│           └── main.go
└── rides-manager
    ├── cmd
    │   └── manager
    │       └── main.go
    └── server.go
```

With exception of the API Server, components only have to be connected to NATS in order to be able to help others finding available drivers. Listing 6-2 shows some of the flags that will be required for the API Server, such as which port to bind the HTTP server to and the endpoint to an available NATS Server.

Listing 6-2. Help Options from API Server

```
$ go run api-server/cmd/api-server/main.go -h
Usage: api-server [options...]

  -help
        Show help
  -listen string
```

```
      Network host:port to listen on (default "0.0.0.0:9090")
  -nats string
      List of NATS Servers to connect (default "nats://
      localhost:4222")
  -version
      Show version
1
```

Listing 6-3 shows a snippet of how to use the Go flag packages for parsing the command-line arguments that are needed for the API Server to run.

Listing 6-3. Flags Definition for the API Server Process

```go
package main

import (
        "flag"
        "fmt"
        "log"
        "os"

        "github.com/nats-io/go-nats"
        "github.com/wallyqs/practical-nats/chapter-06/code/api-
        server"
)

func main() {
        var (
                showHelp      bool
                showVersion   bool
                serverListen  string
                natsServers   string
        )
```

```go
    flag.Usage = func() {
            fmt.Fprintf(os.Stderr, "Usage: api-server
            [options...]\n\n")
            flag.PrintDefaults()
            fmt.Fprintf(os.Stderr, "\n")
    }

    // Setup default flags
    flag.BoolVar(&showHelp, "help", false, "Show help")
    flag.BoolVar(&showVersion, "version", false, "Show
    version")
    flag.StringVar(&serverListen, "listen", "0.0.0.0:9090",
    "Network host:port to listen on")
    flag.StringVar(&natsServers, "nats", nats.DefaultURL,
    "List of NATS Servers to connect")
    flag.Parse()

    switch {
    case showHelp:
            flag.Usage()
            os.Exit(0)
    case showVersion:
            fmt.Fprintf(os.Stderr, "NATS Rider API Server
            v%s\n", apiserver.Version)
            os.Exit(0)
    }
    log.Printf("Starting NATS Rider API Server version %s",
    apiserver.Version)
    // ...
}
```

There is going to be quite a bit of reusable functionality among the components in the system, so as it is convention in Go projects, we will be including the shared piece of functionality in a *kit* package that they can all import.

Defining a Base Component

Inside of the kit package (see Listing 6-4), we will add a Component type that will be holding a collection of functions related to the lifecycle of the NATS connection, along with some other common subscriptions from all components in the system, such as those used for monitoring or help for observability purposes.

Listing 6-4. Defining the Kit Package

```
├── kit
.   └── component
.       └── component.go
```

Listing 6-5 shows how we use the Component to register the API Server in the system and connect to NATS.

Listing 6-5. Registering the API Server as a Component

```go
package main

import (
        // ...
        "github.com/wallyqs/practical-nats/chapter-06/code/kit"
)

func main() {
        // ...
        // Register new component within the system.
        comp := kit.NewComponent("api-server")
```

```
// Connect to NATS and setup discovery subscriptions.
err := comp.SetupConnectionToNATS(natsServers)
if err != nil {
        log.Fatal(err)
}
// ...
}
```

Listing 6-6 shows the type definition for the component. Besides having a connection to NATS, we also want NATS Rider components to be identified by the kind of component they are and an unique identifier string.

Listing 6-6. Reusable Component Type

```
type Component struct {
        // kind is the type of component.
        kind string

        // uuid is a unique identifier sed for this component.
        uuid string

        // nc is the connection to NATS.
        nc *nats.Conn
}
```

In order to generate the unique identifiers, we use the NATS NUID project. It is a high-performance unique identifiers generation library that's also used when making requests with inboxes in the client. Listing 6-7 shows the implementation of the NewComponent function in the kit package to create a component already labeled with an identifier.

Listing 6-7. Labeling Components in the System Using NUID

```
package kit

import (
        "github.com/nats-io/nuid"
)

type Component struct {
        // ...
}

func NewComponent(kind string) *Component {
        return &Component{
                id:   nuid.Next(),
                kind: kind,
        }
}
```

Customizing the Connection to NATS

One important responsibility of the component is that it will have shared functions about handling a NATS connection. Not all the components in the system use the same settings as in Listing 6-8, so we will extend the variadic function parameters that the nats.Connect function can take.

Listing 6-8. The SetupConnectionToNATS Implementation

```
// SetupConnectionToNATS connects to NATS and registers the event
// callbacks and makes it available for discovery requests as well.
func (c *Component) SetupConnectionToNATS(servers string,
options ...nats.Option) error {
```

```
    // Label the connection with the kind and id from
      component.
    options = append(options, nats.Name(c.Name()))

    c.cmu.Lock()
    defer c.cmu.Unlock()

    // Connect to NATS with customized options.
    nc, err := nats.Connect(servers, options...)
    if err != nil {
            log.Fatal(err)
    }
    c.nc = nc
```

Note that we include by default a `nats.Name` for the connection for all the clients in the system, which is useful when enabling monitoring, as shown in the next chapter.

Another thing that all clients should implement are the event handlers from the NATS connection. Listing 6-9 shows how to define the handlers to log reconnection events and errors.

Listing 6-9. Implementing the Event Handlers for the Client

```
func (c *Component) SetupConnectionToNATS(servers string,
options ...nats.Option) error {
  // Handle protocol errors and slow consumer cases
  nc.SetErrorHandler(func(_ *nats.Conn, _ *nats.Subscription,
  err error) {
        log.Printf("NATS Error: %s\n", err)
})
  nc.SetReconnectHandler(func(_ *nats.Conn) {
        log.Println("Reconnected!")
  })
```

```
nc.SetDisconnectHandler(func(_ *nats.Conn) {
    log.Println("Disconnected!")
})
nc.SetClosedHandler(func(_ *nats.Conn) {
    panic("Connection to NATS is closed!")
})
/...
}
```

Enabling Components Discovery

All components that are part of the NATS Rider system should be available
for discovery purposes, as shown in Figure 6-3.

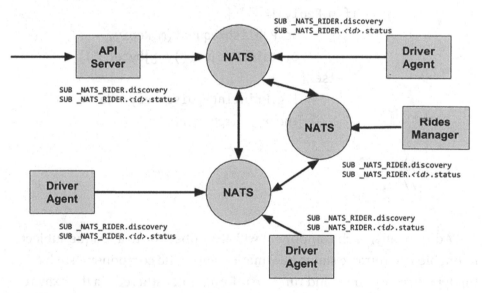

Figure 6-3. *Discovery and status subscriptions*

A NATS Rider component, when connecting to NATS, will subscribe to the _NATS_RIDER.discovery subject which, if sent a request, will make it reply with the unique ID of the component (see Listing 6-10).

Listing 6-10. The SetupConnectionToNATS Reusable Logic

```
func (c *Component) SetupConnectionToNATS(servers string,
options ...nats.Option) error {
        // ...
        // Register component so that it is available for
           discovery requests.
        _, err = c.nc.Subscribe("_NATS_RIDER.discovery", func(m
        *nats.Msg) {
                // Reply directly with own name if requested
                if m.Reply != "" {
                        nc.PublishRequest(m.Reply,
                        c.StatusSubject(), []byte(""))
                } else {
                        log.Println("[Discovery] No Reply
                        inbox, skipping...")
                }
        })
        // ...
}
```

Additionally, each component will also subscribe to a unique subject to enable it to retrieve status information about the component, such as the type of component and runtime information gathered via the expvar package (see Listing 6-11).

Listing 6-11. Status Subscription for Components

```
package kit

import (
        "encoding/json"
        "expvar"
        "fmt"
        "log"
        "runtime"

        "github.com/nats-io/go-nats"
        // ...
)

func (c *Component) SetupConnectionToNATS(servers string,
options ...nats.Option) error {
        // ...
        // Register component so that it is available for
           direct status requests.
        // e.g. _NATS_RIDER.:id.status
        statusSubject := fmt.Sprintf("_NATS_RIDER.%s.status",
        c.id)
        _, err = c.nc.Subscribe(statusSubject, func(m *nats.
        Msg) {
                if m.Reply != "" {
                        log.Println("[Status] Replying with
                        status...")
                        statsz := struct {
                                Kind string       `json:"kind"`
                                ID   string       `json:"id"`
```

```
                          Cmd  []
                          string          `json:"cmdline"`
                          Mem  runtime.MemStats
                          `json:"memstats"`
                  }{
                          Kind: c.kind,
                          ID:   c.id,
                          Cmd:  expvar.Get("cmdline").
                          (expvar.Func)().([]string),
                          Mem:  expvar.Get("memstats").
                          (expvar.Func)().(runtime.
                          MemStats),
                  }
                  result, err := json.Marshal(statsz)
                  if err != nil {
                          log.Printf("Error: %s\n", err)
                          return
                  }
                  nc.Publish(m.Reply, result)
          } else {
                  log.Println("[Status] No Reply inbox,
                  skipping...")
          }
      })
      // ...
}
```

Now, by sending a request to the _NATS_RIDER.discovery subject, it is possible to collect the IDs from all the components from the system and send a request directly to them to gather status information.

Listing 6-12 shows a telnet session making a request to gather all components replies available by using a subscription to an INBOX.example

subject that is later published to the _NATS_RIDER.discovery using
_INBOX.example as the reply subject. Then, it picks the ID that was part of
the payload and uses it to send a status request directly to that component
only (PUB _NATS_RIDER.EtWpbOogWMOFM4Ev7hz3Bx.status _INBOX.
example in the example).

Listing 6-12. Components Discovery via telnet

```
telnet 127.0.0.1 4222
Trying 127.0.0.1...
sub _INBOX.example 1
+OK
pub _NATS_RIDER.discovery _INBOX.example 0
+OK
MSG _INBOX.example 1 22
EtWpbOogWMOFM4Ev7hz3Bx
MSG _INBOX.example 1 22
DxQKFgtFWoOiRmFYaWNvOC
MSG _INBOX.example 1 22
siHky1FQR9Y2Udlacmcejk
PUB _NATS_RIDER.EtWpbOogWMOFM4Ev7hz3Bx.status _INBOX.example 0
+OK
MSG _INBOX.example 1 4684
{"kind":"driver-agent","id":"EtWpbOogWMOFM4Ev7hz3Bx",<rest of
message...>
```

The NATS Rider API

Using the shared component library, we can now introduce the API Server
as the first element of the application. Listing 6-13 shows the full example
of using the component kit package for the API Server.

Listing 6-13. Component Kit Package usage for the API Server

```go
package main
import (
        "flag"
        "fmt"
        "log"
        "os"
        "runtime"

        "github.com/nats-io/go-nats"
        "github.com/wallyqs/practical-nats/chapter-06/code/api-
        server"
        "github.com/wallyqs/practical-nats/chapter-06/code/kit"
)

func main() {
        var (
                showHelp bool
                showVersion bool
                serverListen string
                natsServers string
        )
        flag.Usage = func() {
                fmt.Fprintf(os.Stderr, "Usage: api-server
                [options...]\n\n")
                flag.PrintDefaults()
                fmt.Fprintf(os.Stderr, "\n")
        }

        // Setup default flags
        flag.BoolVar(&showHelp, "help", false, "Show help")
```

```go
flag.BoolVar(&showVersion, "version", false, "Show
version")
flag.StringVar(&serverListen, "listen", "0.0.0.0:9090",
"Network host:port to listen on")
flag.StringVar(&natsServers, "nats", nats.DefaultURL,
"List of NATS Servers to connect")
flag.Parse()

switch {
case showHelp:
        flag.Usage()
        os.Exit(0)
case showVersion:
        fmt.Fprintf(os.Stderr, "NATS Rider API Server
        v%s\n", apiserver.Version)
        os.Exit(0)
}
log.Printf("Starting NATS Rider API Server version %s",
apiserver.Version)

// Register new component within the system.
comp := kit.NewComponent("api-server")

// Connect to NATS and set up discovery subscriptions.
err := comp.SetupConnectionToNATS(natsServers)
if err != nil {
        log.Fatal(err)
}
s := apiserver.Server{
        Component: comp,
}
```

```
        err = s.ListenAndServe(serverListen)
        if err != nil {
                log.Fatal(err)
        }
        log.Printf("Listening for HTTP requests on %v",
        serverListen)
        runtime.Goexit()
}
```

The API Server is the only HTTP Server that is involved in the implementation from NATS Rider, and it exposes a simple API to which the users can make POST requests to be matched against a driver at a location. Listing 6-14 shows the implementation of the ListenAndServe function for the API Server that takes as a parameter the network address and port to which the HTTP server should be binding (by default, it's 0.0.0.0:9090).

Listing 6-14. HTTP Endpoints from the API Server

```
// ListenAndServe takes the network address and port that
// the HTTP server should bind to and starts it.
func (s *Server) ListenAndServe(addr string) error {
        mux := http.NewServeMux()

        // GET /
        mux.HandleFunc("/", func(w http.ResponseWriter,
        r *http.Request) {
                // \See: https://golang.org/pkg/net/
                http/#ServeMux.Handle
                if r.URL.Path != "/" {
                        http.NotFound(w, r)
                        return
                }
```

```
        fmt.Fprintf(w, fmt.Sprintf("NATS Rider API
        Server v%s\n", Version))
})

// POST /rides
mux.HandleFunc("/rides", s.HandleRides)

l, err := net.Listen("tcp", addr)
if err != nil {
        return err
}
srv := &http.Server{
        Addr:           addr,
        Handler:        mux,
        ReadTimeout:    10 * time.Second,
        WriteTimeout:   10 * time.Second,
        MaxHeaderBytes: 1 << 20,
}
go srv.Serve(l)

        return nil
}
```

Each time a POST request is sent to the API Server to /rides, one of the Rides Manager is going to responsible for finding a match to the request (see Figure 6-4).

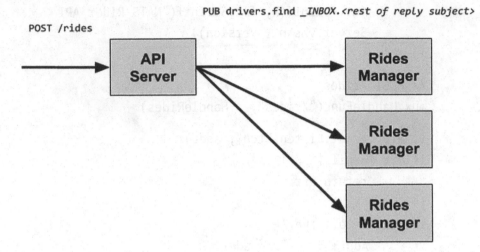

Figure 6-4. *Rides Managers using QueueSubscribe*

In order to handle the requests and responses, we add another piece of shared functionality to the kit package. Listing 6-15 shows the types declarations for the requests and responses that would flow through the system encoded in JSON.

Listing 6-15. Request/Response Types Used by Application

```go
package kit

// Location represents the latitude and longitude pair.
type Location struct {
        // Latitude is the latitude of the user making the
        // request.
        Latitude float64 `json:"lat,omitempty"`

        // Longitude is the longitude of the user making the
        // request.
        Longitude float64 `json:"lng,omitempty"`
}
```

```go
// DriverAgentRequest is the request sent to the driver.
type DriverAgentRequest struct {
        // Type is the type of agent that is requested.
        Type string `json:"type,omitempty"`

        // Location is the location of the user that is being
        // served the request.
        Location *Location `json:"location,omitempty"`

        // RequestID is the ID from the request.
        RequestID string `json:"request_id,omitempty"`
}

// DriverAgentResponse is the response from the driver.
type DriverAgentResponse struct {
        // ID is the identifier of the driver that will accept
        // the request.
        ID string `json:"driver_id,omitempty"`

        // Error is included in case there was an error
        // handling the request.
        Error string `json:"error,omitempty"`
}
```

Listing 6-16 shows the implementation of the HandleRides function from the API Server using these types. Once the HTTP request is received, the API Server will send a NATS request to the drivers.find subject in order to locate a driver that is available to handle the request. Note that it uses the NUID package again in order to tag the request with a tracing ID that will be included in the logs as components handle the request.

Listing 6-16. API Server /rides Handler Implementation

```go
// HandleRides processes requests to find available drivers in
an area.
func (s *Server) HandleRides(w http.ResponseWriter, r *http.
Request) {
        if r.Method != "POST" {
                http.Error(w, "Invalid request method", http.
                StatusMethodNotAllowed)
        }

        body, err := ioutil.ReadAll(r.Body)
        if err != nil {
                http.Error(w, "Bad Request", http.
                StatusBadRequest)
                return
        }

        var request *kit.DriverAgentRequest
        err = json.Unmarshal(body, &request)
        if err != nil {
                http.Error(w, "Bad Request", http.
                StatusBadRequest)
                return
        }

        // Tag the request with an ID for tracing in the logs.
        request.RequestID = nuid.Next()
        req, err := json.Marshal(request)
        if err != nil {
                http.Error(w, "Internal Server Error", http.
                StatusInternalServerError)
                return
```

```go
}
nc := s.NATS()

// Find a driver available to help with the request.
log.Printf("requestID:%s - Finding available driver for
request: %s\n", request.RequestID, string(body))
msg, err := nc.Request("drivers.find", req, 5*time.
Second)
if err != nil {
        log.Printf("requestID:%s - Gave up finding
        available driver for request\n", request.
        RequestID)
        http.Error(w, "Request timeout", http.
        StatusRequestTimeout)
        return
}
log.Printf("requestID:%s - Response: %s\n", request.
RequestID, string(msg.Data))

var resp *kit.DriverAgentResponse
err = json.Unmarshal(msg.Data, &resp)
if err != nil {
        http.Error(w, "Internal Server Error", http.
        StatusInternalServerError)
        return
}
if resp.Error != "" {
        http.Error(w, resp.Error, http.
        StatusServiceUnavailable)
        return
}
```

```
        log.Printf("requestID:%s - Driver with ID %s is
        available to handle the request", request.RequestID,
        resp.ID)
        fmt.Fprintf(w, string(msg.Data))
}
```

Listing 6-17 shows how to start the API Server in its current implementation, assuming that there is an available NATS Server at 127.0.0.1:4222.

Listing 6-17. Starting the API Server

```
$ go run code/api-server/cmd/api-server/main.go -nats
"nats://127.0.0.1:4222"
Starting NATS Rider API Server version 0.1.0
Listening for HTTP requests on 0.0.0.0:9090
```

Since other parts of the system are not ready, making a request will fail with a timeout (see Listing 6-18).

Listing 6-18. Starting the API Server

```
$ curl http://127.0.0.1:9090/
NATS Rider API Server v0.1.0

$ curl http://127.0.0.1:9090/rides -d '{"type":"regular"}'
Request timeout
```

The Load Balanced Rider Manager

The Rides Manager is responsible for dealing with anything related to supporting drivers (see Figure 6-5). Rather than having this logic embedded in the API Server, we avoid having a monolith, as this way the concern of load balancing the work could be offloaded into another service, thus making up for a simpler implementation in the API Server call.

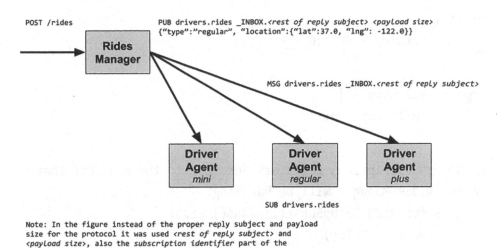

POST /rides   PUB drivers.rides _INBOX.*<rest of reply subject>* *<payload size>*
                     {"type":"regular", "location":{"lat":37.0, "lng": -122.0}}

Rides Manager

MSG drivers.rides _INBOX.*<rest of reply subject>*

Driver Agent *mini*   **Driver Agent** *regular*   **Driver Agent** *plus*

SUB drivers.rides

Note: In the figure instead of the proper reply subject and payload size for the protocol it was used *<rest of reply subject>* and *<payload size>*, also the *subscription identifier* part of the protocol was elided.

Figure 6-5. *Rides Manager finding available drivers*

Listing 6-19 shows an implementation of the Rides Manager consisting of only a single Queue Subscription using the group named manager. Any other node that registers interest into drivers.find and is part of the manager queue group will help load balance the work of finding available drivers that can support the request from the user.

Listing 6-19. Rides Manager Subscriptions

```
package ridesmanager

import (
        "encoding/json"
        "log"
        "time"
```

```go
        "github.com/nats-io/go-nats"
        "github.com/wallyqs/practical-nats/chapter-06/code/kit"
)

const (
        Version = "0.1.0"
)

type Server struct {
        *kit.Component
}

// SetupSubscriptions registers interest to the subjects that
// the Rides Manager will be handling.
func (s *Server) SetupSubscriptions() error {
        nc := s.NATS()

        // Helps finding an available driver to accept a drive
            request.
        nc.QueueSubscribe("drivers.find", "manager", func(msg
        *nats.Msg) {
                var req *kit.DriverAgentRequest
                err := json.Unmarshal(msg.Data, &req)
                if err != nil {
                        log.Printf("Error: %v\n", err)
                        return
                }
                log.Printf("requestID:%s - Driver Find
                Request\n", req.RequestID)
                response := &kit.DriverAgentResponse{}

                // Find an available driver that can handle the
                    user request.
                m, err := nc.Request("drivers.rides", msg.Data,
                2*time.Second)
```

```
if err != nil {
        response.Error = "No drivers available
        found, sorry!"
        resp, err := json.Marshal(response)
        if err != nil {
                log.Printf("requestID:%s -
                Error preparing response: %s",
                        req.RequestID, err)
                return
        }

        // Reply with error response
        nc.Publish(msg.Reply, resp)
        return
}
response.ID = string(m.Data)

resp, err := json.Marshal(response)
if err != nil {
        response.Error = "No drivers available
        found, sorry!"
        resp, err := json.Marshal(response)
        if err != nil {
                log.Printf("requestID:%s -
                Error preparing response: %s",
                        req.RequestID, err)
                return
        }

        // Reply with error response
        nc.Publish(msg.Reply, resp)
        return

}
```

```
                log.Printf("requestID:%s - Driver Find
                Response: %+v\n",
                        req.RequestID, string(m.Data))
                nc.Publish(msg.Reply, resp)
        })

        return nil
}
```

Once it receives the request on `drivers.find`, it will make another request, but this time to `drivers.rides`, which is the subscription being used by the driver agents that are awaiting for requests from users.

Similar to how we did with the API Server, Listing 6-20 shows using the reusable `Component` type that was created to register the Rides Manager.

Listing 6-20. Rides Manager Process

```
package main

import (
        "flag"
        "fmt"
        "log"
        "os"
        "runtime"

        "github.com/nats-io/go-nats"
        "github.com/wallyqs/practical-nats/chapter-06/code/kit"
        "github.com/wallyqs/practical-nats/chapter-06/code/
        rides-manager"
)

func main() {
        var (
                showHelp    bool
```

```
        showVersion bool
        natsServers string
)
flag.Usage = func() {
        fmt.Fprintf(os.Stderr, "Usage: rides-manager
        [options...]\n\n")
        flag.PrintDefaults()
        fmt.Fprintf(os.Stderr, "\n")
}

// Set up default flags
flag.BoolVar(&showHelp, "help", false, "Show help")
flag.BoolVar(&showVersion, "version", false, "Show
version")
flag.StringVar(&natsServers, "nats", nats.DefaultURL,
"List of NATS Servers to connect")
flag.Parse()

switch {
case showHelp:
        flag.Usage()
        os.Exit(0)
case showVersion:
        fmt.Fprintf(os.Stderr, "NATS Rider Rides
        Manager Server v%s\n", ridesmanager.Version)
        os.Exit(0)
}
log.Printf("Starting NATS Rider Rides Manager version
%s", ridesmanager.Version)

comp := kit.NewComponent("rides-manager")
err := comp.SetupConnectionToNATS(natsServers)
if err != nil {
```

```
                log.Fatal(err)
        }

        s := ridesmanager.Server{
                Component: comp,
        }
        err = s.SetupSubscriptions()
        if err != nil {
                log.Fatal(err)
        }

        runtime.Goexit()
}
```

Listing 6-21 shows how to start the Rides Manager to make it available in the system.

Listing 6-21. Starting the Rides Manager

```
$ go run code/rides-manager/cmd/manager/main.go
Starting NATS Rider Rides Manager version 0.1.0
```

The system is not ready yet, so if we send another request, naturally it will fail with an error (see Listing 6-22).

Listing 6-22. Result From Making a Request

```
$ curl -v "http://127.0.0.1:9090/rides" -X POST -d
'{"type": "mini"}'
No drivers available found, sorry
```

The Driver Agent

Finally, this is where it all comes together. Each one of the cars in the service is installed with a lightweight agent that connects to a node in the NATS cluster and makes itself available to receive ride requests. The driver agent will have time to decide whether it is a good, and then the user will expect a single response from the driver who was the fastest and fittest to handle the request. Figure 6-6 shows an example of the flow of a request made to the API Server, which then asks the Rides Manager to find an available driver.

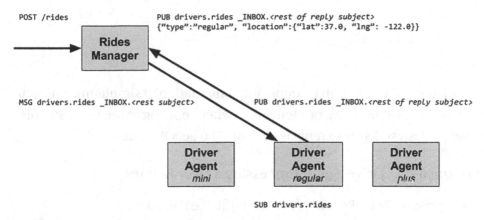

Figure 6-6. *Driver Agent responding to a request*

The Driver Agent will look at each request and check how convenient is it to support the user (for example, it could omit replying if it has different plans soon or delay the reply if it's too far away if a `lat`/`lng` pair was passed in the request). When users make a request, they indicate the type of vehicle that they want, so the Driver Agent will be checking this piece of information and responding appropriately. Listing 6-23 shows the implementation of the agent and how it is setting up the `drives.rides` subscription that's used by the Rides Manager to find available drivers.

Listing 6-23. Driver Agent Subscriptions

```
func (s *Agent) SetupSubscriptions() error {
        nc := s.NATS()

        nc.Subscribe("drivers.rides", func(msg *nats.Msg) {
                if err := processDriveRequest(msg.Data);
                err != nil {
                        log.Printf("Error: %s\n", err)
                        return
                }
        })

        return nil
}
```

Listing 6-24 shows an example implementation of simulating handling a driver request by using random delay when replying to the request. This way, the fastest driver to reply is the one who gets the job.

Listing 6-24. Drive Agent Processing a User Request

```
func processDriveRequest(payload []byte) error {
        var req *kit.DriverAgentRequest
        err := json.Unmarshal(msg.Data, &req)
        if err != nil {
                log.Printf("Error: %v\n", err)
                return err
        }
        log.Printf("requestID:%s - Driver Ride Request:
        type:%s\n",
                req.RequestID, req.Type)
```

```
if req.Type != s.Type() {
        // Skip request since this agent is of a
           different type.
        return nil
}
log.Printf("requestID:%s - Available to handle
request", req.RequestID)

// Random delay agent when receiving drive request
// to simulate latency in replying.
duration := time.Duration(rand.Int31n(1000)) * time.
Millisecond
log.Printf("requestID:%s - Backing off for %s before
replying", req.RequestID, duration)
time.Sleep(duration)

// Replying with own ID meaning that can help.
return s.NATS().Publish(msg.Reply, []byte(s.ID()))
}
```

Listing 6-25 shows the main package for the Driver Agent, which is similar to the API Server and Rides Manager. Note that the agent is using the nats.MaxReconnects(-1) option to set infinite reconnects. This way, it will not stop trying to reconnect to an available server in the cluster, even when it's been disconnected for a long time.

Listing 6-25. Driver Agent Component Setup

```
package main

import (
        "flag"
        "fmt"
        "log"
```

```go
        "os"
        "runtime"

        "github.com/nats-io/go-nats"
        "github.com/wallyqs/practical-nats/chapter-06/code/
        driver-agent"
        "github.com/wallyqs/practical-nats/chapter-06/code/kit"
)

func main() {
        var (
                showHelp    bool
                showVersion bool
                natsServers string
                agentType   string
        )
        flag.Usage = func() {
                fmt.Fprintf(os.Stderr, "Usage: driver-agent
                [options...]\n\n")
                flag.PrintDefaults()
                fmt.Fprintf(os.Stderr, "\n")
        }

        // Set up default flags
        flag.BoolVar(&showHelp, "help", false, "Show help")
        flag.BoolVar(&showVersion, "version", false, "Show
        version")
        flag.StringVar(&natsServers, "nats", nats.DefaultURL,
        "List of NATS Servers to connect")
        flag.StringVar(&agentType, "type", "regular", "Kind of
        vehicle")
        flag.Parse()
```

```go
switch {
case showHelp:
        flag.Usage()
        os.Exit(0)
case showVersion:
        fmt.Fprintf(os.Stderr, "NATS Rider Driver Agent
        v%s\n", driveragent.Version)
        os.Exit(0)
}
log.Printf("Starting NATS Rider Driver Agent version
%s", driveragent.Version)

comp := kit.NewComponent("driver-agent")

// Set infinite retries to never stop reconnecting to
// an available NATS Server in case of an unreliable
   connection.
err := comp.SetupConnectionToNATS(natsServers, nats.
MaxReconnects(-1))
if err != nil {
        log.Fatal(err)
}

ag := driveragent.Agent{
        Component: comp,
        AgentType: agentType,
}
err = ag.SetupSubscriptions()
if err != nil {
        log.Fatal(err)
}

runtime.Goexit()
}
```

Now that the Driver Agent is done, the system is ready to be used. Listing 6-26 shows the process of starting a couple of agents of different types.

Listing 6-26. Running Agents of Different Types

```
$ go run code/driver-agent/cmd/agent/main.go -type mini
Starting NATS Rider Driver Agent version 0.1.0

$ go run code/driver-agent/cmd/agent/main.go -type regular
Starting NATS Rider Driver Agent version 0.1.0
```

If we make a request, we would see in the logs the components cooperating to handle the request (see Listing 6-27).

Listing 6-27. Running Agents of Different Types

```
curl "http://127.0.0.1:9090/rides" -X POST -d
'{"type": "mini"}'
# {"driver_id":"mKFJOZzmawAzaxEKkjKRAP"}

# Component logs
03:30:11 Starting NATS Rider API Server version 0.1.0
03:30:11 Listening for HTTP requests on 0.0.0.0:9090
03:32:25 requestID:RTQDBOPXxGFCES8YCNFZkg - Finding available
driver for request: {"type": "mini"}
03:32:26 requestID:RTQDBOPXxGFCES8YCNFZkg - Response: {"driver_
id":"mKFJOZzmawAzaxEKkjKRAP"}
03:32:26 requestID:RTQDBOPXxGFCES8YCNFZkg - Driver with ID
mKFJOZzmawAzaxEKkjKRAP is available to handle the request

# Rides Manager logs
03:30:15 Starting NATS Rider Rides Manager version 0.1.0
03:32:25 requestID:RTQDBOPXxGFCES8YCNFZkg - Driver Find Request
```

```
03:32:26 requestID:RTQDBOPXxGFCES8YCNFZkg - Driver Find
Response: mKFJOZzmawAzaxEKkjKRAP

# Driver Agent
03:30:16 Starting NATS Rider Driver Agent version 0.1.0
03:32:25 requestID:RTQDBOPXxGFCES8YCNFZkg - Driver Ride
Request: type:mini
03:32:25 requestID:RTQDBOPXxGFCES8YCNFZkg - Available to handle
request
03:32:25 requestID:RTQDBOPXxGFCES8YCNFZkg - Backing off for
727ms before replying
```

Summary

This chapter covered how to develop a simple application using NATS that could be extended to cover more use cases. In the next chapters, we will be using this application a bit to cover important aspects, from operating NATS applications such as monitoring and security, as well as looking at troubleshooting scenarios that may arise in the system.

CHAPTER 7

Monitoring NATS

NATS uses a simple /varz monitoring style after a practice followed at Google.[1] By inspecting the data from the monitoring port from NATS, we can better understand the performance of the system as a whole and make data-based decisions on whether to scale up the services, or to investigate and find bad actors in the system.

In this chapter, we take a look in detail at some of the monitoring options provided by the server, taking as an example the setup from the application that we developed in the previous chapter.

Server Instrumentatlon

When monitoring is enabled in gnatsd, the server embeds an HTTP server so the client can poll the data related to the internal statistics maintained by the server.

The monitoring endpoint from the server can be activated by passing a port to use to the -m or --http_port flags. Listing 7-1 shows an example of starting the server binding the monitoring port to port 8222.

---

[1]More about applications instrumentation at Google: http://landing.google. com/sre/book/chapters/practical-alerting.html

© Waldemar Quevedo 2018
W. Quevedo, *Practical NATS*, https://doi.org/10.1007/978-1-4842-3570-6_7

Listing 7-1. Enabling a Monitoring Port in the Command Line

```
$ gnatsd -m 8222 --logtime=false
[1696] [INF] Starting nats-server version 1.0.4
[1696] [INF] Starting http monitor on 0.0.0.0:8222
[1696] [INF] Listening for client connections on 0.0.0.0:4222
[1696] [INF] Server is ready
```

One of the benefits of this monitoring style is that it takes very little tooling to monitor it; a simple monitoring client could just be a combination of the curl and watch commands together to periodically monitor the state from the server every second, as shown in Listing 7-2.

Listing 7-2. Simple varz-Based Monitoring

```
watch -n 1 curl http://127.0.0.1:8222/varz --silent
```

There are four main endpoints exposed by the server from which we can get instrumentation data—these are the /varz, /connz, /subsz and /routez endpoints.

In the following sections, we take a closer look at the data exposed by each endpoint and learn how to take advantage of the exported data by the server.

The /varz Endpoint

In /varz, it is possible to find overall information about the server, such as the server ID and uptime, its configuration, number of connections, as well as CPU and memory usage.

Listing 7-3 shows a sample of the type of data that can be found in /varz.

Listing 7-3. Sample varz Data

```
$ curl http://127.0.0.1:8222/varz

{
  "server_id": "Mj9vK5hACbgf7u4t8gmXLo",
  "version": "1.1.0",
  "go": "go1.9.2",
  "host": "0.0.0.0",
  "auth_required": false,
  "ssl_required": false,
  "tls_required": false,
  "tls_verify": false,
  "addr": "0.0.0.0",
  "max_connections": 65536,
  "ping_interval": 120000000000,
  "ping_max": 2,
  "http_host": "0.0.0.0",
  "http_port": 8222,
  "https_port": 0,
  "auth_timeout": 1,
  "max_control_line": 1024,
  "cluster": {
    "addr": "0.0.0.0",
    "cluster_port": 0,
    "auth_timeout": 1
  },
  "tls_timeout": 0.5,
  "port": 4222,
  "max_payload": 1048576,
  "start": "2018-02-03T09:03:27.104765-08:00",
  "now": "2018-02-03T09:08:31.693724-08:00",
```

```
  "uptime": "5m4s",
  "mem": 13680640,
  "cores": 4,
  "cpu": 0.3,
  "connections": 17,
  "total_connections": 17,
  "routes": 0,
  "remotes": 0,
  "in_msgs": 0,
  "out_msgs": 0,
  "in_bytes": 0,
  "out_bytes": 0,
  "slow_consumers": 0,
  "subscriptions": 54,
  "http_req_stats": {
    "/": 1,
    "/connz": 302,
    "/routez": 0,
    "/subsz": 0,
    "/varz": 303
  },
  "config_load_time": "2018-02-03T09:03:27.104765-08:00"
}
```

As you can see, many of the fields are related to the current configuration from the server. If there has been a reload operation done to the server (via the HUP signal), there is a config_load_time field that timestamps each time that an operation reload is applied to the running server process.

You can also determine build information about the server, such as the version of the server or even the version of Go used to produce the binary.

On start, the NATS Server will generate a unique identifier to label itself (server_id in the varz data), which can be useful when monitoring a full-mesh cluster in order to identify the server.

The /varz endpoint also includes very important statistics about the performance from the server in its current environment. A snippet of this data can be found in Listing 7-4.

Listing 7-4. Connections Information in varz

```
// ...
"uptime": "5m4s",
"mem": 13680640,
"cores": 4,
"cpu": 0.3,
"connections": 17,
"total_connections": 17,
"routes": 0,
"remotes": 0,
"in_msgs": 0,
"out_msgs": 0,
"in_bytes": 0,
"out_bytes": 0,
"slow_consumers": 0,
"subscriptions": 54,
// ...
```

The slow_consumers entry shown here is particularly important, as it gets incremented whenever there is a client that's connected to NATS but cannot drain the bytes from the socket fast enough. This can possibly impact the service and cause issues in the system. A sudden constant increasing count of slow_consumer can indicate a degradation in performance at some segment of the system, which points to an issue that ought to be addressed.

The memory and cpu being used by the server are also quite important. If the server is starting to use a lot of memory, this could be correlated to the server holding a large number of subscriptions, for example. When having many clients in the server at the same time, there can be bumps in the CPU usage from the server, especially when the clients are using TLS.

The in_msgs/out_msgs fields are statistics kept by the server and are related to how many messages have been sent to the server by a client (in_msgs) and how many messages the server has delivered to clients that had registered an interest in the subject (out_msgs).

Similarly, the in_bytes/out_bytes fields hold information about how many bytes have been published to the server and the total size of the messages being delivered to the clients so far.

In the nats-io/go-nats repository, there is a nats-bench tool that can be used to confirm the throughput from a NATS Server in a certain environment. By using the varz data, we can inspect the status of the benchmark as it progresses (see Listing 7-5).

Listing 7-5. Messages Throughput in /varz

```
$ watch -n 1 'curl http://127.0.0.1:8222/varz --silent | grep
"\(msgs\|byte\)"'
...
  "in_msgs": 70000000,
  "out_msgs": 0,
  "in_bytes": 40000000,
  "out_bytes": 0,

$ cd src/github.com/nats-io/go-nats
$ go run examples/nats-bench.go -np 20 -n 10000000 -ms 1 hi
Starting benchmark [msgs=10000000, msgsize=0, pubs=20, subs=0]
Pub stats: 10,037,294 msgs/sec ~ 9.57 MB/sec
...
```

The /connz Endpoint

The /connz endpoint holds statistics and metadata about the clients currently connected to the server. Listing 7-6 shows an example of the sample data that we get via /connz.

Listing 7-6. Sample connz Data

```
$ curl http://127.0.0.1:8222/connz
{
  "now": "2018-02-04T10:36:53.33824-08:00",
  "num_connections": 17,
  "total": 17,
  "offset": 0,
  "limit": 1024,
  "connections": [
    {
      "cid": 1,
      "ip": "127.0.0.1",
      "port": 49307,
      "start": "2018-02-04T10:23:59.387138-08:00",
      "last_activity": "2018-02-04T10:23:59.387545-08:00",
      "uptime": "12m53s",
      "idle": "12m53s",
      "pending_bytes": 0,
      "in_msgs": 0,
      "out_msgs": 0,
      "in_bytes": 0,
      "out_bytes": 0,
      "subscriptions": 4,
      "name": "rides-manager:GPPt15ETRM5cm3ECaLOzpx",
      "lang": "go",
```

```
    "version": "1.3.1"
  },
  ...
  ]
}
```

Similar to when using varz, you can find the in/out messages and bytes that have been flowing through the client (see Listing 7-7):

- out_msgs/out_bytes are the number of messages and bytes that the client has received (that is whenever the clients gets a MSG from the protocol)

- in_msgs/in_bytes are the number of messages and bytes that the client has sent (increments every time that the client sends PUB)

Listing 7-7. In/Out Messages and Bytes from a Client

```
"in_msgs": 0,
"out_msgs": 0,
"in_bytes": 0,
"out_bytes": 0,
```

By convention, all clients that connect to a NATS Server should be announcing the current version of the client and its language when sending CONNECT to the server. As part of the CONNECT payload, it is also possible to give the client a name, which if combined with a unique identifier, can be useful to discern the role or type of component connected to NATS.

None of these fields is strictly necessary, but if the client has sent them, the fields will be included by the server as part of the metadata that the server holds about the client (see Listing 7-8).

Listing 7-8. Info from Connected Client

```
"name": "rides-manager:GPPt15ETRM5cm3ECaLOzpx",
"lang": "go",
"version": "1.3.1"
```

Whenever a client connects to the server, it will label it with a connection ID (CID), which combined with tracing or debug logging in the server, can be useful for investigating the behavior of a client in handling a message.

Listing 7-9 shows an example of a couple of clients named sub and pub that are receiving and publishing messages, respectively. In the example, the pub connection will send 10 messages and then stop.

Listing 7-9. Pair of Named Clients Publishing and Receiving Messages

```
package main

import (
        "log"
        "runtime"

        "github.com/nats-io/go-nats"
)

func main() {
        nc1, err := nats.Connect("nats://127.0.0.1:4222",
        nats.Name("sub"))
        if err != nil {
                log.Fatal(err)
        }
        nc2, err := nats.Connect("nats://127.0.0.1:4222",
        nats.Name("pub"))
```

```go
    if err != nil {
        log.Fatal(err)
    }
    nc2.Subscribe("example", func(m *nats.Msg) {
        log.Printf("[Received] %s\n", string(m.Data))
    })

    for i := 0; i < 10; i++ {
        nc1.Publish("example", []byte("hello"))
    }
    nc1.Flush()
    runtime.Goexit()
}
```

Running the example and looking at the results after making a request to /connz (see Listing 7-10), we can notice that the client named sub has in_msgs set to 10, and the client named pub has out_msgs set to 10.

Listing 7-10. In/Out Msgs Monitoring in /connz

```
$ go run code/pub-sub-test.go
^Z

$ curl http://127.0.0.1:8222/connz

{
  "server_id": "HewfTLSkp9YaxzjmyXxmSr",
  "now": "2018-03-27T16:18:17.457613123-07:00",
  "num_connections": 2,
  "total": 2,
  "offset": 0,
  "limit": 1024,
  "connections": [
```

```json
{
  "cid": 3,
  "ip": "127.0.0.1",
  "port": 50032,
  "start": "2018-03-27T16:06:57.663295386-07:00",
  "last_activity": "2018-03-27T16:06:57.664432684-07:00",
  "uptime": "11m19s",
  "idle": "11m19s",
  "pending_bytes": 0,
  "in_msgs": 10,
  "out_msgs": 0,
  "in_bytes": 50,
  "out_bytes": 0,
  "subscriptions": 0,
  "name": "sub",
  "lang": "go",
  "version": "1.3.1"
},
{
  "cid": 4,
  "ip": "127.0.0.1",
  "port": 50033,
  "start": "2018-03-27T16:06:57.663971404-07:00",
  "last_activity": "2018-03-27T16:06:57.664432684-07:00",
  "uptime": "11m19s",
  "idle": "11m19s",
  "pending_bytes": 0,
  "in_msgs": 0,
  "out_msgs": 10,
  "in_bytes": 0,
  "out_bytes": 50,
```

```
      "subscriptions": 1,
      "name": "pub",
      "lang": "go",
      "version": "1.3.1"
    }
  ]
}
```

Showing Client Subscriptions

It is hidden by default, but there is an extra level of verbosity that can be enabled in the /connz endpoint in order to get the list of subscriptions of each client.

In order to do this, we use the special query parameter subs. Listing 7-11 shows a curl client making a request using /connz?subs=1 and running clients from the application that was developed in the previous chapter.

Listing 7- 11. Toggling Client Subscriptions

```
$ curl http://127.0.0.1:8222/connz?subs=1

{
  "now": "2018-02-04T11:41:02.54257-08:00",
  "num_connections": 17,
  "total": 17,
  "offset": 0,
  "limit": 1024,
  "connections": [
    {
      "cid": 1,
      ...
      "name": "api-server:4BSSBvCeckW3TyqKiWR9Ic",
      ...
```

```
    "subscriptions_list": [
      "_NATS_RIDER.discovery",
      "_NATS_RIDER.*.4BSSBvCeckW3TyqKiWR9Ic.status",
      "_INBOX.4BSSBvCeckW3TyqKiWR9Js.*"
    ]
  },
  {
    "cid": 2,
    ...
    "name": "driver-agent:o874B2pmEzEjZOTeAfXJsb",
    ...
    "subscriptions_list": [
      "drivers.rides",
      "_NATS_RIDER.discovery",
      "_NATS_RIDER.*.o874B2pmEzEjZOTeAfXJsb.status"
    ]
  },
  {
    "cid": 3,
    ...
    "name": "rides-manager:1WnIh1N9QnHkHT6XL1EMZ6",
    ...
    "subscriptions_list": [
      "_NATS_RIDER.discovery",
      "_NATS_RIDER.*.1WnIh1N9QnHkHT6XL1EMZ6.status",
      "drivers.find",
      "_INBOX.1WnIh1N9QnHkHT6XL1EMZr.*"
    ]
  },
  ...
  ]
}
```

You will notice that in the response payload, there is now a subscriptions_list field that includes the collection of subscriptions, to which each one of the clients has registered interest.

Sorting and Limiting Query Results

If there are too many clients connected to the server, getting all the data available related to the client connections might be too noisy for investigation purposes. In order to help with this, the /connz endpoint supports the query parameters limit and offset in order to narrow down the results being returned by the server.

By default, the list of connections provided by the server is ordered in order of CID. This means that if we query for a single connection, result is going to be oldest connection established to the server. Listing 7-12 shows an example of making a request to the monitoring port and limiting a single result. You can notice that, as part of the response, there are 17 total connections, but the field num_connections is set to 1 since we are only getting a single entry due to the limit.

Listing 7-12. Limiting Results from /connz

```
$ curl 'http://127.0.0.1:8222/connz?limit=1'
{
  "now": "2018-02-04T14:32:06.808218-08:00",
  "num_connections": 1,
  "total": 17,
  "offset": 0,
  "limit": 1,
  "connections": [
    {
      "cid": 1,
      "ip": "127.0.0.1",
      "port": 52119,
```

```
    "start": "2018-02-04T11:23:52.84029-08:00",
    "last_activity": "2018-02-04T11:24:44.686233-08:00",
    "uptime": "1h49m39s",
    "idle": "1h48m47s",
    "pending_bytes": 0,
    "in_msgs": 3,
    "out_msgs": 3,
    "in_bytes": 24,
    "out_bytes": 66,
    "subscriptions": 3,
    "name": "api-server:4BSSBvCeckW3TyqKiWR9Ic",
    "lang": "go",
    "version": "1.3.1"
  }
 ]
}
```

From the previous response, we already know that there are 17
connections established to the server. In Listing 7-13, it is shown that
it is possible to skip the first 16 connections and instead get the oldest
connection established to NATS. We do this by combining it with the
offset and limit it to a single connection to be included in the response.

Listing 7-13. Skipping Entries in /connz

```
$ curl 'http://127.0.0.1:8222/connz?limit=1&offset=16'
{
  "now": "2018-02-04T14:31:48.354052-08:00",
  "num_connections": 1,
  "total": 17,
  "offset": 16,
  "limit": 1,
  "connections": [
```

```
    {
      "cid": 17,
      "ip": "127.0.0.1",
      "port": 52134,
      "start": "2018-02-04T11:23:52.864348-08:00",
      "last_activity": "2018-02-04T11:24:46.344434-08:00",
      "uptime": "1h49m20s",
      "idle": "1h48m27s",
      "pending_bytes": 0,
      "in_msgs": 10,
      "out_msgs": 10,
      "in_bytes": 220,
      "out_bytes": 80,
      "subscriptions": 3,
      "name": "driver-agent:OzgeYwhzBbtK9xZLgzDvOU",
      "lang": "go",
      "version": "1.3.1"
    }
  ]
}
```

If the offset is set to be more than the number of connections, the result will be an empty list.

We can decide to sort by a different key as well by using the sort query parameter. Using subs as the sorting option, we can request the top connection that has the most subscriptions. An example of this usage is shown in Listing 7-14, where it is limiting to get a single result using subs as the key for sorting.

Listing 7-14. Combining Sorts and Limit

```
$ curl 'http://127.0.0.1:8222/connz?subs=1&sort=subs&limit=1'
{
  "now": "2018-02-04T16:19:54.517079-08:00",
  "num_connections": 1,
  "total": 17,
  "offset": 0,
  "limit": 1,
  "connections": [
    {
      "cid": 4,
      "ip": "127.0.0.1",
      "port": 52123,
      "start": "2018-02-04T11:23:52.851202-08:00",
      "last_activity": "2018-02-04T11:24:46.762113-08:00",
      "uptime": "3h37m26s",
      "idle": "3h36m33s",
      "pending_bytes": 0,
      "in_msgs": 6,
      "out_msgs": 36,
      "in_bytes": 90,
      "out_bytes": 750,
      "subscriptions": 4,
      "name": "rides-manager:CTaLprNj7pONtJLBoLJ2Mr",
      "lang": "go",
      "version": "1.3.1",
      "subscriptions_list": [
        "_INBOX.CTaLprNj7pONtJLBoLJ2Ok.*",
        "_NATS_RIDER.discovery",
```

```
        "_NATS_RIDER.*.CTaLprNj7pONtJLBoLJ2Mr.status",
        "drivers.find"
    ]
  }
 ]
}
```

Other sorting options include `cid` (the default), `subs`, `msgs_to`, `msgs_from`, `bytes_to`, `bytes_from`, `last`, `idle`, `pending`, and `uptime`.

In Listing 7-15, we can find an example of getting the top client that has received the most messages. From the results, we can see that in this case it is one of the Rider Managers from the previous chapter who has been receiving the most messages. Remember that we were using a queue subscription for load balancing here, but the message is delivered randomly to one of the members in the group. That means there is a chance for one of them to have received a slightly higher number of messages than others in the same group.

Listing 7-15. Query for Connection Sending the Most Messages

```
$ curl 'http://127.0.0.1:8222/connz?subs=1&sort=msgs_
to&limit=1'
{
  "now": "2018-02-04T16:30:48.617634-08:00",
  "num_connections": 1,
  "total": 17,
  "offset": 0,
  "limit": 1,
  "connections": [
    {
      "cid": 14,
      "ip": "127.0.0.1",
      "port": 52132,
```

```
"start": "2018-02-04T11:23:52.860447-08:00",
"last_activity": "2018-02-04T11:24:45.974665-08:00",
"uptime": "3h48m21s",
"idle": "3h47m27s",
"pending_bytes": 0,
"in_msgs": 10,
"out_msgs": 60,
"in_bytes": 150,
"out_bytes": 1250,
"subscriptions": 4,
"name": "rides-manager:GPPt15ETRM5cm3ECaLOzpx",
"lang": "go",
"version": "1.3.1",
"subscriptions_list": [
  "_NATS_RIDER.discovery",

  "_NATS_RIDER.*.GPPt15ETRM5cm3ECaLOzpx.status",
  "drivers.find",
  "_INBOX.GPPt15ETRM5cm3ECaLOzsa.*"
]
}
]
}
```

About /routez

The /routez endpoint was mentioned briefly in the chapter about clustering. If you have a pool of NATS Servers running as a cluster, this endpoint can be useful for detecting the current status of the client connections from the mesh.

Let's say, for example, that we start a cluster, as shown in Listing 7-16.

Listing 7-16. Assembling a Three-Node NATS Cluster

```
SERVERS=nats://127.0.0.1:6222,nats://127.0.0.1:6223,na
ts://127.0.0.1:6224
gnatsd -V -T -p 4222 -m 8222 -cluster nats://127.0.0.1:6222
-routes $SERVERS &
gnatsd -V -T -p 4223 -m 8223 -cluster nats://127.0.0.1:6223
-routes $SERVERS &
gnatsd -V -T -p 4224 -m 8224 -cluster nats://127.0.0.1:6224
-routes $SERVERS &
```

After having some clients connect to the cluster, we can inspect the state of the cluster from the perspective of the first node (see Listing 7-17).

Listing 7-17. Inspecting /routez Data

```
$ curl http://127.0.0.1:8222/routez
{
  "now": "2018-02-04T17:36:32.942303-08:00",
  "num_routes": 2,
  "routes": [
    {
      "rid": 1,
      "remote_id": "akWIfPhuz3TgKJ4rLjVngy",
      "did_solicit": true,
      "is_configured": true,
      "ip": "127.0.0.1",
      "port": 6224,
      "pending_size": 0,
      "in_msgs": 0,
      "out_msgs": 0,
      "in_bytes": 0,
```

```
      "out_bytes": 0,
      "subscriptions": 9
    },
    {
      "rid": 4,
      "remote_id": "up4vD1A8eyWxwmZinOKtLy",
      "did_solicit": true,
      "is_configured": true,
      "ip": "127.0.0.1",
      "port": 6223,
      "pending_size": 0,
      "in_msgs": 0,
      "out_msgs": 0,
      "in_bytes": 0,
      "out_bytes": 0,
      "subscriptions": 45
    }
  ]
}
```

The routes from a NATS cluster themselves act as clients internally. Similar to the /connz endpoint, in Listing 7-18 it is passed subs as a query parameter when making the request in order to get the list of the subscriptions that the routes are holding.

Listing 7-18. Inspecting Subscriptions from /routez

```
$ curl http://127.0.0.1:8222/routez?subs=1
{
  "now": "2018-02-04T18:08:07.478325-08:00",
  "num_routes": 2,
  "routes": [
```

```
{
  "rid": 1,
  "remote_id": "akWIfPhuz3TgKJ4rLjVngy",
  "did_solicit": true,
  "is_configured": true,
  "ip": "127.0.0.1",
  "port": 6224,
  "pending_size": 0,
  "in_msgs": 0,
  "out_msgs": 0,
  "in_bytes": 0,
  "out_bytes": 0,
  "subscriptions": 9,
  "subscriptions_list": [

    "_NATS_RIDER.*.OUoJyU8iSgjJhlIeEwEXnz.status",
    "_NATS_RIDER.discovery",

    "_NATS_RIDER.*.9oRlB5JkjM2SgvXc2BDzyX.status",
    "drivers.rides",
    "_NATS_RIDER.discovery",
    "_NATS_RIDER.discovery",
    "_NATS_RIDER.*.OJtAPcUHxCFTpbvePnzatB.status",
    "drivers.rides",
    "drivers.rides"
  ]
},
{
  "rid": 4,
  "remote_id": "up4vD1A8eyWxwmZinOKtLy",
  "did_solicit": true,
  "is_configured": true,
```

```
    "ip": "127.0.0.1",
    "port": 6223,
    "pending_size": 0,
    "in_msgs": 0,
    "out_msgs": 0,
    "in_bytes": 0,
    "out_bytes": 0,
    "subscriptions": 45,
    "subscriptions_list": [

        "_NATS_RIDER.*.yrEbwPREXu7UtvA8rtQtve.status",
        "drivers.find",
        "_INBOX.mEAbzfIoZ3n6AOKlMxDnzA.*",

        "_NATS_RIDER.*.4BSSBvCeckW3TyqKiWR9Ic.status",

        "_NATS_RIDER.*.dI85VMkQS23OtJZ4oOQ22l.status",
        ...
        "_NATS_RIDER.discovery",
        "drivers.rides",
        "_NATS_RIDER.discovery"
    ]
  }
 ]
}
```

Again, for the cluster to work properly, all members in the cluster should eventually have two routes in order for the full-mesh to exist. When we're deploying a NATS cluster and we know the static list of IPs and ports from servers in the cluster, one way to confirm that the NATS service is available is by checking whether each one of the servers has the proper number of routes established already (see Listing 7-19).

Listing 7-19. Ensuring a Cluster Is Fully Formed

```
for port in 8222 8223 8224; do
  curl http://127.0.0.1:$port/routez | grep num_routes
done
  "num_routes": 2,
  "num_routes": 2,
  "num_routes": 2,
```

If that is not the case, there might be an issue with the formation of the cluster and there might be a partition. The messages will not be routed properly.

About /subsz

This endpoint provides cumulative stats about the internal state of the sublist data structure that the server maintains (see Listing 7-20). For admin purposes, the data presented might be too advanced, so using /subsz is handier when making improvements to the server implementation.

Listing 7-20. Sublist Structure Internal Data

```
$ curl http://127.0.0.1:8222/subsz
{
  "num_subscriptions": 54,
  "num_cache": 2,
  "num_inserts": 54,
  "num_removes": 0,
  "num_matches": 140,
  "cache_hit_rate": 0.9857142857142858,
  "max_fanout": 0,
  "avg_fanout": 0
}
```

The `num_subscriptions` is essentially the same information that can be found in the `/varz` endpoint, so when we are monitoring the server, it is not strictly necessary to get the information from here.

Using nats-top for Monitoring

The NATS team maintains a small utility that can be used to inspect the current state of the connections to the server. It's called `nats-top` (see `https://github.com/nats-io/nats-top`).

To install it, you can use `go get` to get the latest `nats-top` binary compiled for your platform, as shown in Listing 7-21.

Listing 7-21. Installing nats-top

```
# Installing nats-top via go get
go get github.com/nats-io/nats-top
```

The `nats-top` utility is an example of a simple client that can be built that feeds from the data of the server. By default, it will try to connect to the 8222 monitoring port from a locally available gnatsd process, but by using the `-s` and `-m` flags, we can modify the address and monitoring port of the server, as demonstrated in Listing 7-22.

Listing 7-22. Connecting to the Monitoring Port with nats-top

```
$ nats-top -s 127.0.0.1 -m 8223
```

Once it's running, we get in the terminal an overview of the state of each client that is connected to that particular NATS Server (see Listing 7-23).

Listing 7-23. Example nats-top Output

```
NATS server version 1.1.0 (uptime: 51m42s)
Server:
  Load: CPU:  0.0% Memory: 14.3M  Slow Consumers: 0
  In:   Msgs: 12.5K  Bytes: 249.6K  Msgs/Sec: 0.0
  Out:  Msgs: 19.6K  Bytes: 306.7K  Msgs/Sec: 0.0

Connections Polled: 14
```

HOST	CID	SUBS	MSGS_TO	MSGS_FROM
192.168.1.9:60703	7	3	913	913
192.168.99.1:60685	8	3	913	913
192.168.1.9:60686	9	3	913	913
192.168.99.1:60689	10	3	304	304
192.168.1.9:60692	11	3	305	305
192.168.99.1:60693	12	3	913	913
192.168.99.1:60694	13	3	913	913
192.168.99.1:60695	14	3	913	913
192.168.1.9:60698	15	4	3.7K	632
192.168.99.1:60699	16	3	913	913
192.168.1.9:60701	17	3	913	913
192.168.1.9:60707	18	4	3.6K	620
192.168.99.1:60713	19	4	3.4K	574
192.168.1.9:60710	20	3	304	304

By default, the list of connections will be sorted by CID, but by pressing the letter O, it is possible to set a different sorting option. Listing 7-24 shows some of the other options available in nats-top. This help message can be displayed in your terminal by pressing ?.

Listing 7-24. A nats-top Help Message

```
Command      Description

o<option>    Set primary sort key to <option>.

             Option can be one of: {cid|subs|pending|msgs_
             to|msgs_from|
             bytes_to|bytes_from|idle|last}

             This can be set in the command line too with -sort
             flag.

n<limit>     Set sample size of connections to request from the
             server.

             This can be set in the command line as well via -n
             flag.
             Note that if used in conjunction with sort, the
             server
             would respect both options allowing queries like
             'connection
             with largest number of subscriptions': -n 1 -sort
             subs

s            Toggle displaying connection subscriptions.

d            Toggle activating DNS address lookup for clients.

q            Quit nats-top.
```

We can sort by the number of messages that have been received (msgs_to) and get a different result as well. In Listing 7-25, we can see that the Rider Manager components are the ones that have received the most messages.

Listing 7-25. Sorting Functions in nats-top

```
NATS server version 1.0.4 (uptime: 59m11s)
Server:
  Load: CPU:  0.0%  Memory: 14.3M  Slow Consumers: 0
  In:   Msgs: 12.5K  Bytes: 249.6K  Msgs/Sec: 0.0
  Out:  Msgs: 19.6K  Bytes: 306.7K  Msgs/Sec: 0.0

Connections Polled: 14
  HOST                   CID  SUBS  MSGS_TO  MSGS_FROM
  192.168.1.9:60698      15   4     3.7K     632
  192.168.1.9:60707      18   4     3.6K     620
  192.168.99.1:60713     19   4     3.4K     574
  192.168.99.1:60693     12   3     913      913
  192.168.1.9:60686      9    3     913      913
  192.168.1.9:60703      7    3     913      913
  192.168.99.1:60694     13   3     913      913
  192.168.99.1:60695     14   3     913      913
  192.168.1.9:60701      17   3     913      913
  192.168.99.1:60699     16   3     913      913
  192.168.99.1:60685     8    3     913      913
  192.168.1.9:60692      11   3     305      305
  192.168.99.1:60689     10   3     304      304
  192.168.1.9:60710      20   3     304      304
```

Summary

In this chapter, we covered some of the important aspects of monitoring a NATS Server. In case you might be using Prometheus as part of your setup, the NATS team also maintains an exporter which transforms the server metrics into Prometheus format (available at `https://github.com/natsio/prometheus-nats-exporter`). In the next chapters, we take a look at how to make our deployment more secure by using certificates and enabling TLS in the cluster.

CHAPTER 8

Securing NATS

In the early chapters of this book, we mentioned that NATS has as its main core values not only simplicity and performance but also *security*. The NATS project values ease of use a lot, and protocol being in plain text helps a lot for debugging and inspecting raw traffic without many complications, but these benefits lose value unless we can have our setup secure against attacks from bad actors.

In this chapter, you will learn:

- How NATS handles secure connections to the server

- How to set up TLS for clients to connect securely to the server

- How to set up TLS for a NATS clustering setup

- How to secure the monitoring port from the server

Connecting Securely to NATS

The original Ruby server had some initial support for TLS, but its usage did not evolve a lot as the core EventMachine implementation had some limitations in its TLS support. Fortunately, thanks to the Go rewrite of the server, NATS can take advantage of the mature TLS tooling available in Go and provide first class support to security features. Thus there is no need to compile the server against OpenSSL for example as NATS utilizes the native support built into Go in its crypto/tls package (https://golang.org/pkg/crypto/tls/).

© Waldemar Quevedo 2018
W. Quevedo, *Practical NATS*, https://doi.org/10.1007/978-1-4842-3570-6_8

Establishing a secure connection starts the same way as an insecure connection but clients, after reading the first INFO message from the server, start the TLS handshake to upgrade the connection and continue communicating securely after that.

When a NATS Server is set up to be secure, it will force for all communications to be done in a secure way. In Listing 8-1, a telnet client is trying to establish a connection to the secure port from the demo.nats.io endpoint. Once connected, the server will announce to the client that a secure connection is required and give it some time to establish the connection securely.

Listing 8-1. Attempting to Connect to Secure Server Setup

```
$ telnet demo.nats.io 4443
INFO {..., "ssl_required":true, "tls_required":true,
"tls_verify":false,...}
```

You may notice that there are two similar fields in the initial INFO message—ssl_required and tls_required. The former can be ignored for newer clients, as is related to backward compatibility with the previous implementation of the Ruby server. Newer clients like the Go implementation just check for the presence of tls_required setting to start the TLS handshake.

By default, the server will give the client two seconds to complete securing the connection; otherwise, the client will receive a protocol error message and then the server will close the connection (see Listing 8-2).

Listing 8-2. Timeout When Connecting to NATS

```
$ telnet demo.nats.io 4443
INFO {..., "ssl_required":true, "tls_required":true,
"tls_verify":false,...}
-ERR 'Secure Connection - TLS Required'
```

Once the TLS handshake has been completed, the client will proceed to send the CONNECT command and continue communicating with the server following the NATS protocol in the same way as it was described in Chapter 2. In Figure 8-1, you can find a picture of the overall flow of establishing a secure connection to NATS.

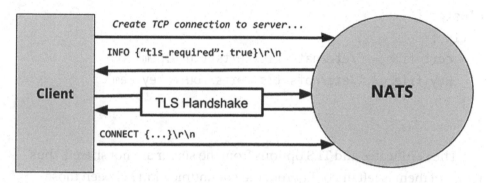

Figure 8-1. *Establishing a secure NATS connection*

Configuring TLS in the Server

It is recommended to configure TLS for NATS by using the configuration file. Reasons for this are outlined in the caveats sections at the end of this chapter, so for the following sections, we only show how to do it via the config file first.

When configuring TLS in NATS, we need to keep in mind that there are actually two different TLS configuration blocks required to fully secure the NATS infrastructure—one TLS block for securing the connections to the clients and another for securing the routes. Listing 8-3 shows an example configuration file containing these two blocks.

Listing 8-3. Server TLS and Routes TLS Configuration Blocks

```
tls {
  cert_file = "/etc/nats-tls/certs/server.pem"
  key_file  = "/etc/nats-tls/certs/server-key.pem"
}

cluster {
  tls {
    cert_file = "/etc/nats-tls/certs/route.pem"
    key_file  = "/etc/nats-tls/certs/route-key.pem"
  }
}
```

The certificates and TLS options from the server are not shared, thus if one of them is left unconfigured, the communication between those endpoints will not be encrypted. Thus there are three things in total that need to be secured:

- The communication between the NATS clients and the NATS Server

- The communication between the NATS Servers with other NATS Servers

- The monitoring port

In the following sections, we take a look at how to set up each one. At the end, we provide a thorough example of having a secure infrastructure from scratch by creating our own CA and certificates.

Securing the Monitoring Endpoint

Enabling monitoring for the server can be done using the -m flag, but there is also a secure version that can be enabled by using -ms (see Listing 8-4).

Listing 8-4. Enabling Secure Monitoring Port

```
gnatsd -ms 8222 -c nats.conf
```

Tuning the Authorization Timeout

Depending on the infrastructure, it might be required to tune the default timeout for TLS handshake (which is by default two seconds). If required, the default timeout can be configured by the tls block stanza in the configuration file. Listing 8-5 shows how to change this timeout to wait five seconds instead.

Listing 8-5. Extending the TLS Timeout

```
tls {
  cert_file = "/etc/nats-tls/certs/server.pem"
  key_file  = "/etc/nats-tls/certs/server-key.pem"
  ca_file   = "/etc/nats-tls/certs/ca.pem"
  verify    = false
  timeout   = 5 # seconds
}
```

Setting a Certificate Authority

In case we are using self-signed certificates (as we will be doing in rest of this chapter), it is necessary to set up the CA against which to validate the certificates with the ca_file option (see Listing 8-6).

Listing 8-6. TLS Using a Custom CA

```
tls {
  cert_file = "/etc/nats-tls/certs/server.pem"
  key_file  = "/etc/nats-tls/certs/key.pem"
  ca_file   = "/etc/nats-tls/certs/cert.new.pem"
}
```

Require Clients to Provide a Certificate

It is possible to force the clients to provide a certificate when establishing a connection to the server by toggling verify to true (see Listing 8-7).

Listing 8-7. TLS Certificate Required Clients

```
tls {
  cert_file = "/etc/nats-tls/certs/server.pem"
  key_file  = "/etc/nats-tls/certs/server-key.pem"
  ca_file   = "/etc/nats-tls/certs/ca.pem"
  verify    = true
}
```

Setting Up a Secure NATS Environment from Scratch

In the following section, we create a secure configuration for NATS from scratch, as shown in Figure 8-2. We create our own CA certificates and use self-signed certificates to demonstrate how a secure setup looks.

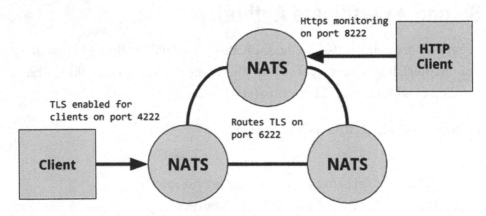

Figure 8-2. *A secure NATS infrastructure*

Installing cfssl for Certs Creation

For the creation of certificates, we will be using the cfssl tool maintained by Cloudflare (`https://github.com/cloudflare/cfssl`). Assuming you already have a working Go environment in order to run previous examples, so you can run go get, as shown in Listing 8-8, to install cfssl on your system.

Listing 8-8. Getting cfssl

```
$ go get -u github.com/cloudflare/cfssl/cmd/cfssl
cfssl version
Version: 1.2.0
Revision: dev
Runtime: go1.9
```

Otherwise, in OSX it is also possible to get it via Homebrew, as shown in Listing 8-9.

Listing 8-9. Installing cfssl via Homebrew

```
$ brew install cfssl
```

Defining the Security Roles

We start by creating the profiles (see Listing 8-10) for the different security roles that are involved:

- *Server*: The server certificate sent to the client

- *Client*: The client certificate sent to the server (since we require clients to send a certificate)

- *Route*: The server certificate used for the full-mesh if using a clustering setup

Listing 8-10. JSON Configuration for Roles (certs/ca-config.json)

```json
{
    "signing": {
        "default": {
            "expiry": "43800h"
        },
        "profiles": {
            "server": {
                "expiry": "43800h",
                "usages": [
                    "signing",
                    "key encipherment",
                    "server auth"
                ]
            },
            "client": {
                "expiry": "43800h",
                "usages": [
                    "signing",
                    "key encipherment",
                    "client auth"
                ]
            },
            "route": {
                "expiry": "43800h",
                "usages": [
                    "signing",
                    "key encipherment",
                    "server auth",
                    "client auth"
                ]
            }
```

```
            }
         }
      }
}
```

Creating a Custom Root CA

We will be setting up our own CA for using self-signed certificates
(see Listing 8-11).

Listing 8-11. Custom Root CA Example (certs/ca-csr.json)

```
{
    "CN": "My Custom CA",
    "key": {
        "algo": "rsa",
        "size": 2048
    },
    "names": [
        {
            "C": "US",
            "L": "CA",
            "O": "My Company",
            "ST": "San Francisco",
            "OU": "Org Unit 1"
        }
    ]
}
```

We will be storing all of these artifacts in a `certs` folder. Running the
`cfssl`, as shown in Listing 8-12, will generate the `ca.pem` file that we will
use to determine the root CA.

Listing 8-12. Generating the CA Certificate

```
cd certs
cfssl gencert -initca ca-csr.json | cfssljson -bare ca -
```

Securing the Connections from the Clients

The first step for security will be creating a certificate for the server that will be used for the client's connections and the monitoring port. In Listing 8-13, you can find a configuration to generate a wildcard certificate for
*.nats-cluster.my-domain.com.

Listing 8-13. Certs for Securing Client Connections

```
{
    "CN": "nats server",
    "hosts": [
        "*.nats-cluster.my-domain.com",
        "nats-cluster.my-domain.com"
    ],
    "key": {
        "algo": "rsa",
        "size": 2048
    },
    "names": [
        {
            "C": "US",
            "L": "CA",
            "ST": "San Francisco"
        }
    ]
}
```

Then we generate the server private key and certificate with `cfssl`, as shown in Listing 8-14.

Listing 8-14. Generating the CA Certificate

```
cd certs
cfssl gencert -ca=ca.pem -ca-key=ca-key.pem -config=ca-config.
json -profile=server server.json | cfssljson -bare server
```

We also require the clients to provide their own certificate, so we need certificates for them as well (see Listings 8-15 and 8-16).

Listing 8-15. Certs to Verify Clients

```
{
    "CN": "nats client",
    "hosts": [""],
    "key": {
        "algo": "rsa",
        "size": 2048
    },
    "names": [
        {
            "C": "US",
            "L": "CA",
            "ST": "San Francisco"
        }
    ]
}
```

Listing 8-16. Generating Clients Certs

```
cd certs
# Generating NATS client certs
cfssl gencert -ca=ca.pem -ca-key=ca-key.pem -config=ca-config.
json -profile=client client.json | cfssljson -bare client
```

Then there is the configuration for the cluster, as shown in Listing 8-17.

Listing 8-17. Configuration to Secure Client Connections

```
tls {
  cert_file = './certs/server.pem'
  key_file =  './certs/server-key.pem'
  ca_file = './certs/ca.pem'
  verify = true

  timeout = 5
}
```

Securing the Monitoring Endpoint

This one is easy since we already have the server certificates. Now we only need to include the https_port into the configuration, as shown in Listing 8-18.

Listing 8-18. Enabling Secure Monitoring Port

```
https_port = 8222

tls {
  cert_file = './certs/server.pem'
  key_file =  './certs/server-key.pem'
  ca_file = './certs/ca.pem'
  verify = true

  timeout = 5
}
```

Securing the Routes from the Cluster

This part is a bit more involved. For the TLS setup of the routes in a cluster, we create a wildcard certificate using a `nats-cluster-route` subdomain under which each one of the nodes will have its own A record. Figure 8-3 shows an image of how it may look.

nats-C.nats-cluster.my-domain.com

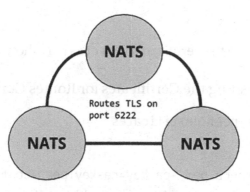

nats-A.nats-cluster.my-domain.com   nats-B.nats-cluster.my-domain.com

Figure 8-3. *TLS for NATS routes*

We start by creating a wildcard certificate for the servers, as shown in Listing 8-19.

Listing 8-19. Wildcard Certificate for Routes

```
{
    "CN": "nats route",
    "hosts": [
        "*.nats-cluster-route.my-domain.com",
    ],
    "key": {
        "algo": "rsa",
        "size": 2048
```

209

```
    },
    "names": [
        {
            "C": "US",
            "L": "CA",
            "ST": "San Francisco"
        }
    ]
}
```

Then we generate the certificates with cfssl, as shown in Listing 8-20.

Listing 8-20. Creating the Certificates for Routes Connections

```
# Generating the peer certificates

cd certs
cfssl gencert -ca=ca.pem -ca-key=ca-key.pem -config=ca-config.
json -profile=route route.json | cfssljson -bare route
```

Now the completed configuration will look like Listing 8-21. Note that we are using an explicit list of the servers under the routes section, using the full A record for each one of the servers (more on that on the TLS caveats section).

Listing 8-21. Enabling TLS for Routes Connections

```
tls {
  cert_file = './certs/server.pem'
  key_file  = './certs/server-key.pem'
  ca_file = './certs/ca.pem'
  timeout = 5
}
```

```
https_port = 8222

cluster {

  tls {
    cert_file = './certs/route.pem'
    key_file =  './certs/route-key.pem'
    ca_file = './certs/ca.pem'

    timeout = 5
  }

  routes = [
    nats://nats-A.nats-cluster-route.my-domain.com:6222
    nats://nats-B.nats-cluster-route.my-domain.com:6222
    nats://nats-C.nats-cluster-route.my-domain.com:6222
  ]

}
```

Caveats from NATS TLS Support

In this section, we cover a few of the common gotchas to keep in mind when deploying NATS clustering with TLS enabled. Note that some of these issues may be resolved in the next few releases, depending on their priority.

Not Possible to Use TLS Right Away

As of latest release v1.0.4, it is not possible to set the clients to use a TLS connection from the start, meaning that features like SNI are currently not supported.[1]

---

[1]GitHub Issue: https://github.com/nats-io/gnatsd/issues/291

The reason for this is that the initial INFO message has to be consumed by the client in plain text, then once it detects that the tls_required is signaling the client to start the secure connection, only then does the TLS handshake negotiation start. Due to this issue, the following will never work, as shown in Listing 8-22.

Listing 8-22. Trying to Connect with openssl Client

```
$ openssl s_client -connect demo.nats.io:4443
```

If you're considering using a load balancer for example, this should be kept in mind since if the load balancer requires a TLS connection from the beginning, you might need to rearchitect a different solution around this limitation.

Limitations of Configuring TLS from the Command Line

As of release v1.0.4, it is currently not possible to apply TLS configuration reload via the HUP signal unless a configuration file is specified. Trying to do so will result in an error appearing in the server logs.

Another issue is that it is only possible to configure the TLS options for the server connections with the clients (the help message can be seen in Listing 8-23). If we're only setting the flags shown in Listing 8-23, the traffic in between the server routes will continue to be in plaintext.

Listing 8-23. TLS Command-Line Options

```
Usage: gnatsd [options]

TLS Options:
        --tls                   Enable TLS, do not verify
                                clients (default: false)
        --tlscert <file>         Server certificate file
```

```
    --tlskey <file>            Private key for server
                               certificate
    --tlsverify                Enable TLS, verify client
                               certificates
    --tlscacert <file>         Client certificate CA for
                               verification
Cluster Options:
    --routes <rurl-1, rurl-2>  Routes to solicit and connect
    --cluster <cluster-url>    Cluster URL for solicited routes
    --no_advertise <bool>      Advertise known cluster IPs to
                               clients
    --connect_retries <number> For implicit routes, number of
                               connect retries
```

Auto Discovery and Routes TLS

If the the server binds to 0.0.0.0, the server will resolve the addresses to send via the INFO protocol. Let's say for example that we have added a new nats-C node to an already formed two-node cluster, as shown in Figure 8-4.

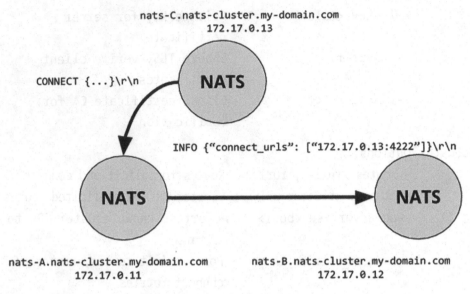

Figure 8-4. Secure NATS cluster with A records

Once the nats-C server connects to the nats-A server, it will announce to nats-B that a new server joined the cluster and that it should connect to it to form the full-mesh. It then sends nats-C the resolved IP address (see Figure 8-4).

Then nats-B will try to connect to nats-C, but if we're using auto-discovery with TLS enabled, we may find the error shown in Listing 8-24 in the logs during autodiscovery (see Figure 8-5).

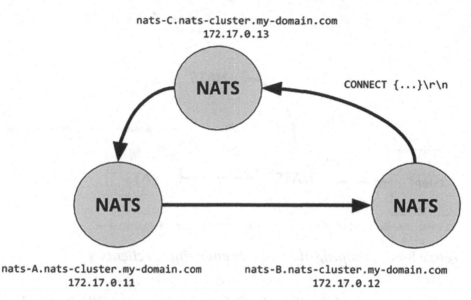

Figure 8-5. *Autodiscovery-based cluster formation*

Listing 8-24. Autodiscovery Gossips IPs via the INFO Protocol

[ERR] 127.0.0.1:6222 - rid:14 - TLS route handshake error:
x509: cannot validate certificate for 127.0.0.1 because it
doesn't contain any IP SANs

Consequently, the clients would also get a list of the resolved IPs or a hostname of the servers in the cluster, as shown in Figure 8-6.

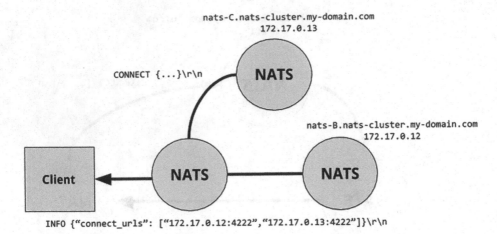

Figure 8-6. *Gossiping of available endpoints to clients*

Starting version 1.0.6 of the NATS Server, it is also possible to provide both the -cluster_advertise and client_advertise options, which allow you to control what the endpoint is that is announced to clients and peers in the network.

Summary

In this chapter, we learned about how to secure our infrastructure so that we have control over which actors are part of the system as well some of the few gotchas that may arise while doing so. Some of these may improve in the next releases, so, as always, feedback is very welcome by the NATS team to help in prioritizing. In the following chapters, we'll take a look at finding solutions to some other gotchas or troubleshooting scenarios that you may run into when using NATS.

CHAPTER 9

Troubleshooting NATS

Although NATS is very simple to operate and offers very strong invariants regarding service stability, it is still needed to keep in mind having the right balance between producers and consumers. Otherwise the service can run into slow consumer issues (looking at NATS as a nervous system helps put the correct mindset around this problem).

In this chapter, you will learn about:

- Different types of *slow consumer* scenarios

- How to tackle slow consumer errors

- Using event callbacks to prevent slow consumers

Types of Slow Consumer Errors

A *slow consumer* is a condition reached by a NATS client where the client is not being able to keep up with the pace at which the NATS Server is sending the messages on which it registered interest.

There are two types of slow consumer error conditions that can be reached:

- Condition A: When the client is not draining from the socket the messages that the server is sending.

© Waldemar Quevedo 2018
W. Quevedo, *Practical NATS*, https://doi.org/10.1007/978-1-4842-3570-6_9

- Condition B: When a single subscription is accumulating too many messages and reaching a buffering limit set in the client.

When condition A occurs (see Figure 9-1), the server will acknowledge this by sending an ERR protocol message to the client before disconnecting the client from the server.

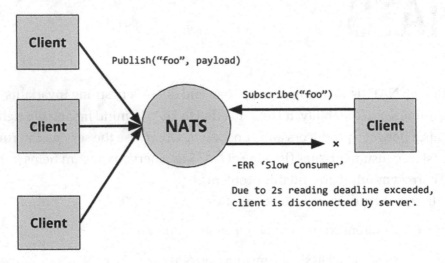

Figure 9-1. *Slow consumer protocol error*

Condition B, on the other hand (see Figure 9-2), is reached when the client has already read the messages from the socket but is not processing them fast enough so that *internally* the client is now buffering a lot of them.

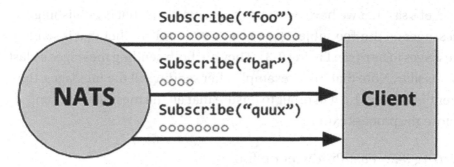

Figure 9-2. *Subscriptions with a slow consumer state*

In the following sections, we describe a bit further both types of scenarios and what strategies can be taken in order to mitigate them.

Troubleshooting Slow Consumer Protocol Errors

Whenever there is a slow consumer protocol error event, the NATS Server will increase its internal counter in order to keep track of the total amount of slow consumers that there have been so far in the server. Listing 9-1 shows how to confirm this from the monitoring endpoint by checking the counter displayed on /varz.

Listing 9-1. Checking Slow Consumers from /varz

```
$ curl http://127.0.0.1:8222/varz | grep slow_consumers
  "slow_consumers": 0,
```

A healthy service should have none or a low count of slow consumers, a large number of them is definitely not good.

We have seen in other chapters examples of reproducing a slow consumer scenario under a tight loop, but this time let's reproduce the issue by splitting the subscribers and publisher into different processes.

219

Let's say that we have two types of clients—one that is publishing messages on the foo subject (see Listing 9-2) and another that is sending messages to bar (see Listing 9-3). They are both sending messages as fast as possible. Note that in the example after sending all the messages, the client is calling Flush in order to ensure that all the messages are sent before the process exits.

Listing 9-2. Fast Producer on foo

```
package main

import (
        "log"

        "github.com/nats-io/go-nats"
)

func main() {
        nc, err := nats.Connect("nats://127.0.0.1:4222")
        if err != nil {
                log.Fatalf("Error: %s", err)
        }

        msg := make([]byte, 1024)
        for i := 0; i < 1024; i++ {
                msg = append(msg, 'A')
        }

        for i := 0; i < 100000000; i++ {
                nc.Publish("foo", msg)
        }
        nc.Flush()
}
```

Listing 9-3. Fast Producer on bar

```go
package main

import (
        "log"

        "github.com/nats-io/go-nats"
)

func main() {
        nc, err := nats.Connect("nats://127.0.0.1:4222")
        if err != nil {
                log.Fatalf("Error: %s", err)
        }

        msg := make([]byte, 128)
        for i := 0; i < 1024; i++ {
                msg = append(msg, 'B')
        }

        for i := 0; i < 100000000; i++ {
                nc.Publish("bar", msg)
        }
        nc.Flush()
}
```

Then we have a subscriber (see Listing 9-4) that has registered interest in the foo and bar subjects, but that whenever it receives a message on foo, it has to do a significant amount of processing before handling the next message.

Listing 9-4. Causing a Slow Consumer with a Tight Loop

```
package main

import (
        "log"

        "github.com/nats-io/go-nats"
)

func main() {
        nc, err := nats.Connect("nats://127.0.0.1:4222")
        if err != nil {
                log.Fatalf("Error: %s", err)
        }
        nc.Subscribe("foo", func(_ *nats.Msg) {
                // Heavy processing
                for i := 0; i < 10000000000; i++ {
                }
        })
        nc.Subscribe("bar", func(_ *nats.Msg) {
                // Not heavy processing
        })
        select {}
}
```

Running a single subscriber and publishers in parallel (see Listing 9-5) will make the subscriber run into a slow consumer error in the server very soon.

Listing 9-5. Running Publisher and Slow Consumer Subscriber

```
# Subscribe to foo and bar
go run slow-consumer-protocol-error-sub-1.go
```

```
# Publish on foo
go run slow-consumer-protocol-error-pub-foo-1.go
```

```
[INF] Starting nats-server version 1.1.0
[INF] Starting http monitor on 127.0.0.1:8222
[INF] Listening for client connections on 127.0.0.1:4222
[INF] Server is ready
[INF] 127.0.0.1:55289 - cid:1 - Slow Consumer Detected
```

In the NATS clients, it is good practice to set the event callbacks, as they will give much better insight around what is the condition that was reached by the client. In Listing 9-6, it is shown how to define all the handlers for the subscription.

Listing 9-6. Setting Up Event Handlers for Debugging

```go
package main

import (
        "log"

        "github.com/nats-io/go-nats"
)

func main() {
        nc, err := nats.Connect("nats://127.0.0.1:4222",
                nats.DisconnectHandler(func(nc *nats.Conn) {
                        log.Printf("Got disconnected!\n")
                }),
                nats.ReconnectHandler(func(nc *nats.Conn) {
```

```
                    log.Printf("Got reconnected to %v!\n",
                    nc.ConnectedUrl())
            }),
            nats.ClosedHandler(func(nc *nats.Conn) {
                    log.Printf("Connection closed. Reason:
                    %v\n", nc.LastError())
            }),
            nats.ErrorHandler(func(nc *nats.Conn,
            sub *nats.Subscription, err error) {
                    log.Printf("Error: %s\n", err)
            }),
    )
    if err != nil {
            log.Fatalf("Error: %s", err)
    }
    nc.Subscribe("foo", func(_ *nats.Msg) {
            // Heavy processing
            log.Println("Start processing 'foo' message")
            for i := 0; i < 10000000000; i++ {
            }
            log.Println("Done processing 'foo' message")
    })
    nc.Subscribe("bar", func(_ *nats.Msg) {
            // Not heavy processing
    })
    select {}
}
```

Now with added logging, we can see that the client is becoming disconnected and reconnected several times (the results are shown in Listing 9-7).

Listing 9-7. Disconnection Events Logged in Callbacks

```
2018/02/28 00:48:27 Start processing 'foo' message
2018/02/28 00:48:37 Done processing 'foo' message
2018/02/28 00:48:37 Start processing 'foo' message
2018/02/28 00:48:37 Got disconnected!
2018/02/28 00:48:37 Got reconnected to nats://127.0.0.1:4222!
2018/02/28 00:48:44 Done processing 'foo' message
2018/02/28 00:48:44 Start processing 'foo' message
```

Although the server may have sent a slow consumer error back to the client, the error callback was so further behind in the processing that it may have missed the server who was trying to send the event to the client.

Clearly a single NATS client would not be able to sustain this amount of traffic. In a real world scenario, when reaching this condition there would be a number of timeouts appearing if there were being requests being made during that time. In order to share the load of an attack, QueueSubscribe could be used instead (see Figure 9-3). Then there would be more workers available to handle the requests and prevent timeouts.

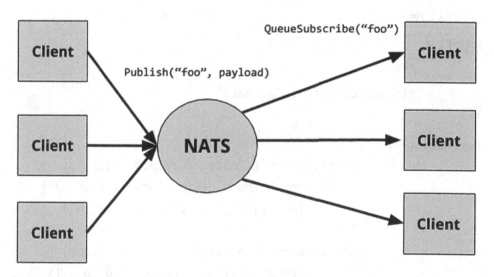

Figure 9-3. *Slow consumer protocol error*

Reaching the point where the client is disconnected due to reaching the slow consumer might be too late to handle and too difficult to control as well. Instead, we can rely on the engine from the client and the internal queues to detect this earlier.

Subscriptions in Slow Consumer State

Since this is an asynchronous subscription that takes a callback, the client will be reading the messages from the socket and internally creating a linked list of up to 65536 messages by default.

The size of this queue of messages can be further controlled by calling SetPendingLimits on the subscription (see Listing 9-8). Reducing the limit to 8192 messages will make it faster for the client to reach the slow consumer state so that, in the error handler, it can be controlled for example to stop receiving messages in the subscription temporarily and let other workers handle instead.

Listing 9-8. Modifying PendingLimits from a Subscription

```
package main

import (
        "log"

        "github.com/nats-io/go-nats"
)

func main() {
        nc, err := nats.Connect("nats://127.0.0.1:4222",
                nats.DisconnectHandler(func(nc *nats.Conn) {
                        log.Printf("Got disconnected!\n")
                }),
                nats.ReconnectHandler(func(nc *nats.Conn) {
                        log.Printf("Got reconnected to %v!\n",
                        nc.ConnectedUrl())
```

```go
        }),
        nats.ClosedHandler(func(nc *nats.Conn) {
                log.Printf("Connection closed. Reason:
                %v\n", nc.LastError())
        }),
        nats.ErrorHandler(func(nc *nats.Conn, sub
        *nats.Subscription, err error) {
                log.Printf("Error: %s\n", err)
                if err == nats.ErrSlowConsumer {
                        log.Printf("Removing subscription
                        on %q\n", sub.Subject)
                        sub.Unsubscribe()
                }
        }),
)
if err != nil {
        log.Fatalf("Error: %s", err)
}
sub, _ := nc.Subscribe("foo", func(_ *nats.Msg) {
        // Heavy processing
        log.Println("Start processing 'foo' message")
        for i := 0; i < 10000000000; i++ {
        }
        log.Println("Done processing 'foo' message")
})
sub.SetPendingLimits(8192, 8192*1024)

nc.Subscribe("bar", func(_ *nats.Msg) {
        // Not heavy processing
})
select {}
}
```

Now as part of the logic of the client, it will be eagerly removing interest in the subject that is causing the client to become a slow consumer (see Listing 9-9). This way, the other subscription bar is not going to be impacted and the worker can still do other tasks other than processing the messages from foo.

Listing 9-9. Detecting Subscription Becoming a Slow Consumer

```
2018/02/28 01:55:44 Error: nats: slow consumer, messages dropped
2018/02/28 01:55:44 Removing subscription on "foo"
2018/02/28 01:55:58 Done processing 'foo' message
```

Routes as Slow Consumers in a NATS Cluster

It is important to keep in mind that when in a clustered NATS setup, the connections from the full-mesh topology can also run into slow consumer scenarios, just like a regular NATS client would.

In case one of the nodes in the cluster cannot drain the messages that the other nodes are routing to it fast enough, the remote client connection will also time out. It will be exceeding the reading deadline, will send the slow consumer protocol error, and then be disconnected (see Figure 9-4).

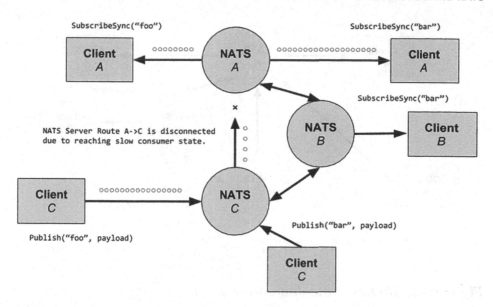

Figure 9-4. *Routes in slow consumer state*

In Figure 9-4, you can see that the NATS Server A has two clients connected to it on the foo and bar subjects and that Servers B and C are routing messages from local clients to those nodes into Server A. In this example, one of the clients local to the NATS Server C is a fast producer and is sending messages to the foo subject as fast as possible. In case the cluster reaches a condition such that the NATS Server C has to route a large number of messages at a pace at which the NATS Server A cannot sustain, the NATS Server C will disconnect the NATS Server A from the cluster. This will indirectly affect another client connected to the NATS Server A, which was sending messages on the bar subject, even if there was no slow consumer scenario related to that subscription (see Figure 9-5).

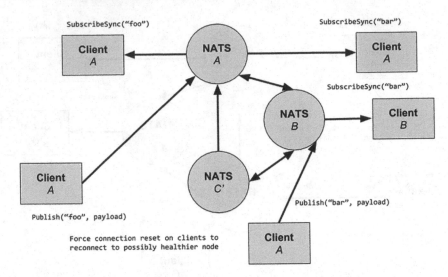

Figure 9-5. *Routes in the slow consumer state*

After being disconnected, Server C will continuously try to reestablish the route connection but will similarly be logging errors related to the consumer state.

If this was a temporary spike, the cluster might eventually recover and proceed as normal, but the condition is still worth monitoring further. One way to keep track of the situation in the cluster is by periodically checking the /routez endpoint from the server as well (see Listing 9-10).

Listing 9-10. Routez Setup in the Public demo.nats.io Endpoint

```
$ curl http://demo.nats.io:8222/routez
{
  "num_routes": 2,
  ...
}
```

For a three-node cluster, each node should always have two routes established, so in case one of the nodes is continuously getting disconnected, it is worth taking a look at the host on which the server is being disconnected. Check where it's located or possibly replace it with a new one. Increasing the cluster size is another option as well, although keep in mind that scaling up the cluster will not necessarily cause a rebalancing of the client connections. Therefore, in order to do so, you might need to restart or replace the server.

Summary

In this chapter, we covered some of the most common error conditions to which a NATS Server can reach because of an imbalance in the communication flow. You may recognize some of the problems covered in this chapter as topics that are usually found in domains such as queuing theory and congestion control. Having a strategy around rate limiting and capacity planning are still important problems that have to be thought out when architecting applications to use NATS. What is great about NATS here is that, while you are scheming a solution on how to handle these scenarios, the NATS Server will always try to improve the guarantees and make sure that the service is reliable and available for clients.

CHAPTER 10

Advanced NATS Techniques

At this point you are already very familiar with the core APIs from NATS and how they can be used to implement messaging-based approaches to communicate with a system. The Publish, Subscribe, and Request APIs may be very simple, but when they're used in combination, we can implement very powerful techniques that solve many problems using NATS.

In this chapter, we take a look at a number of advanced styles of using the NATS client that can help you further squeeze functionality out of NATS.

Using Inbox Subscriptions

We have previously seen that at the core of the Request API lies the unique subscriptions that ensure that the client that is making the request will be the only one receiving the response. Depending on whether the consumer is using QueueSubscribe or bare Subscribe, the message might be received by one or more subscribers in the system. However, remember that as a publisher, we cannot assume the audience and tell exactly whether the message is going to be processed or attempted to be processed at all.

© Waldemar Quevedo 2018
W. Quevedo, *Practical NATS*, https://doi.org/10.1007/978-1-4842-3570-6_10

Listing 10-1 shows an example of a request, where we know that the response may take a long time to process, so we have explicitly bounded the request to use a long timeout of 30 seconds.

Listing 10-1. A Long Request

```go
package main

import (
        "log"
        "time"

        "github.com/nats-io/go-nats"
)
func main() {
        nc, err := nats.Connect(nats.DefaultURL)
        if err != nil {
                log.Fatal(err)
        }

        payload := []byte("hi...")
        log.Println("[Request]", string(payload))
        reply, err := nc.Request("very.long.request", payload,
        30*time.Second)
        if err != nil {
                log.Fatal(err)
        }
        log.Println("[Response]", string(reply.Data))
}
```

In this example, we simulate that the processing of the message will take a long time per request to the subscriber by having a sleep of 20 seconds per message. Remember that a single handler will process each message sequentially, so if we have multiple messages at roughly the same time, each message will be delayed by 20 seconds (see Listing 10-2) unless we increase the number of subscribers.

Listing 10-2. Subscriber with Slow Replies

```
package main

import (
        "log"
        "time"

        "github.com/nats-io/go-nats"
)

func main() {
        nc, err := nats.Connect(nats.DefaultURL)
        if err != nil {
                log.Fatal(err)
        }
        nc.Subscribe("very.long.request", func(m *nats.Msg) {
                log.Println("[Processing]", string(m.Data))
                time.Sleep(20 * time.Second)
                nc.Publish(m.Reply, []byte("done!"))
        })

        log.Println("[Started]")
        select {}
}
```

Although this may work initially, the situation is not ideal since there are many error conditions on which the result of making the request will be reported as a `nats: timeout` error. For example, some of these could be:

- If no subscriber was available to process the message.

- If a subscriber was processing it, but took too long in doing so.

- If a subscriber was available and started processing the message, but did not finish because its process failed.

In comparison, when making an HTTP request, some of these error conditions would have resulted in connection reset or timeout errors against the remote HTTP server, thus making it possible to better discern the failure condition from those type of errors. However, since in NATS, the connection is being brokered by the server, we have to take a different approach.

In the current state, if we try to make the request with no available subscribers, both requestors would time out after 30 seconds (see Listing 10-3).

Listing 10-3. Requestor Timing Out

```
seq 2 | parallel -j 2 -u go run very-long-request-1.go
2018/02/20 14:02:44 [Request] hi...
2018/02/20 14:02:44 [Request] hi...
2018/02/20 14:03:14 nats: timeout
2018/02/20 14:03:14 nats: timeout
exit status 1
```

One possible way to address this issue is to create an extra subscription that the subscribers can announce so that a requestor can first check whether there is a subscriber that could help process the request by making a request with a shorter timeout. Then, once there has been a response, we make the request that is going to take a lot of time to be processed.

By using the nats.NewInbox API, as shown in Listing 10-4, we can create this extra unique subscription that is going to be handling the first step, which is to quickly signal the client that there is at least a single consumer that is available to process the message. Then the old logic, whereby the processing of the message was taking a lot of time, will be moved under that extra subscription.

Listing 10-4. Using an Extra Inbox Subscription

```
package main

import (
        "log"
        "time"

        "github.com/nats-io/go-nats"
)

func main() {
        nc, err := nats.Connect(nats.DefaultURL)
        if err != nil {
                log.Fatal(err)
        }
        myInbox := nats.NewInbox()
        nc.Subscribe("very.long.request", func(m *nats.Msg){
                log.Println("[Processing] Announcing own
                inbox...")
                nc.PublishRequest(m.Reply, myInbox, []byte(""))
        })
```

```
    nc.Subscribe(myInbox, func(m *nats.Msg){
            log.Println("[Processing] Message:", string(m.
            Data))
            time.Sleep(20 * time.Second)
            nc.Publish(m.Reply, []byte("done!"))
    })

    log.Println("[Started]")
    select {}
}
```

Then on the requestor side, we make two requests (see Listing 10-5). The first one is with a shorter timeout to be able to determine whether there is another subscriber available to process the request. Then there is another request where the requestor will send directly to the inbox that was announced by the subscriber as a response from the original request.

Listing 10-5. Leveraging Unique Subscriptions for Requests

```
package main

import (
        "log"
        "time"

        "github.com/nats-io/go-nats"
)

func main() {
        nc, err := nats.Connect(nats.DefaultURL)
        if err != nil {
                log.Fatal(err)
        }
```

```go
log.Println("[Inbox Request]")
reply, err := nc.Request("very.long.request", []
byte(""), 5*time.Second)
if err != nil {
        log.Fatalf("No nodes available to reply: %s",
        err)
}
inbox := reply.Reply
log.Println("[Detected node]", inbox)

payload := []byte("hi...")
response, err := nc.Request(inbox, payload, 30*time.
Second)
if err != nil {
        log.Fatal(err)
}

log.Println("[Response]", string(response.Data))
}
```

With these changes, now if there are no available consumers, we would detect that the service is not available much faster and switch to a different type of logic (see Listing 10-6).

Listing 10-6. Running a Requestor That Times Out

```
$ go run very-long-request-2.go
2018/02/20 14:09:49 [Inbox Request]
2018/02/20 14:09:54 No nodes available to reply: nats: timeout
exit status 1
```

For the next step, let's start the subscribers that are going to be following this new request protocol to better detect that the service is available before processing the message (see Listing 10-7).

Listing 10-7. Running Multiple Subscribers in Parallel

```
$ seq 10 | parallel -j 10 -u go run long-request-subscriber-2.
go
2018/02/20 14:17:15 [Started]
2018/02/20 14:17:16 [Started]
...

$ seq 2 | parallel -j 2 -u go run very-long-request-2.go
2018/02/20 14:17:19 [Inbox Request]
2018/02/20 14:17:19 [Detected node] _INBOX.
C2Tzbe1Lg3MvJSymTbrk9d
2018/02/20 14:17:19 [Inbox Request]
2018/02/20 14:17:19 [Detected node] _
INBOX.87wQLqFGsgZ4hgYrwHdV5B
2018/02/20 14:17:39 [Response] done!
2018/02/20 14:17:39 [Response] done!
```

As it is right now, each request is broadcasted to all the publishers, so there is still a chance that some of the requests will time out. We can improve this a bit by considering whether the node is currently working by the time it handled the request for an inbox (see Listing 10-8).

Listing 10-8. Backing Off When Busy in Subscriber

```go
package main

import (
        "log"
        "time"

        "sync"

        "github.com/nats-io/go-nats"
)
```

```go
func main() {
        var busy bool
        var l sync.Mutex
        nc, err := nats.Connect(nats.DefaultURL)
        if err != nil {
                log.Fatal(err)
        }
        myInbox := nats.NewInbox()
        nc.Subscribe("very.long.request", func(m *nats.Msg) {
                l.Lock()
                shouldSkip := busy
                l.Unlock()

                // Only reply when not busy
                if shouldSkip {
                        return
                }

                log.Println("[Processing] Announcing own
                inbox...")
                nc.PublishRequest(m.Reply, myInbox, []byte(""))
        })

        nc.Subscribe(myInbox, func(m *nats.Msg) {
                log.Println("[Processing] Message:",
                string(m.Data))
                l.Lock()
                busy = true
                l.Unlock()
                time.Sleep(20 * time.Second)

                l.Lock()
                busy = false
```

```
                l.Unlock()
                nc.Publish(m.Reply, []byte("done!"))
        })

        log.Println("[Started]")
        select {}
}
```

Taking into account whether the subscriber is busy handling a request before accepting further requests decreases the chance that a time out will occur. A couple more improvements that could be done is to use QueueSubscribe for the *very.long.request* topic in order to load balance the traffic, as shown in Listing 10-9. We could also make it possible to signal to the requestor quickly that the consumer that got the request is not able to process it.

Listing 10-9. Using QueueSubscribe for Load Balancing

```
package main

import (
        "log"
        "time"

        "sync"

        "github.com/nats-io/go-nats"
)

func main() {
        var busy bool
        var l sync.Mutex
        nc, err := nats.Connect(nats.DefaultURL)
        if err != nil {
                log.Fatal(err)
        }
```

```go
myInbox := nats.NewInbox()
nc.QueueSubscribe("very.long.request", "workers",
func(m *nats.Msg) {

        l.Lock()
        shouldSkip := busy
        l.Unlock()

        // Only reply when not busy
        if shouldSkip {
                // Reply with empty inbox to signal
                that
                // was not available to process
                request.
                nc.PublishRequest(m.Reply, "", []
                byte(""))
                return
        }

        log.Println("[Processing] Announcing own
        inbox...")
        nc.PublishRequest(m.Reply, myInbox, []byte(""))
})

nc.Subscribe(myInbox, func(m *nats.Msg) {
        log.Println("[Processing] Message:",
        string(m.Data))
        l.Lock()
        busy = true
        l.Unlock()
        time.Sleep(20 * time.Second)

        l.Lock()
        busy = false
```

```
                l.Unlock()
                nc.Publish(m.Reply, []byte("done!"))
        })

        log.Println("[Started]")
        select {}
}
```

Since NATS will be sending a message to one of the subscribers randomly, if one of the consumers of the message is busy handling the message, the client can retry a few times so that its request is processed by a subscriber that is available.

Listing 10-10 shows an example of adding retry logic to try to get a subscriber that can help before sending the request.

Listing 10-10. Retries for an Available Subscriber

```
package main

import (
        "log"
        "time"

        "github.com/nats-io/go-nats"
)

func main() {
        nc, err := nats.Connect(nats.DefaultURL)
        if err != nil {
                log.Fatal(err)
        }

        var i int
        var inbox string
        for ; i < 5; i++ {
```

```
            log.Println("[Inbox Request]")
            reply, err := nc.Request("very.long.request",
            []byte(""), 5*time.Second)
            if err != nil {
                    log.Println("Retrying...")
                    continue
            }
        if reply.Reply == "" {
                    log.Println("Node replied with empty
                    inbox, retry again later...")
                    time.Sleep(1 * time.Second)
                    continue
        }

            inbox = reply.Reply
            break
    }
    if i == 5 {
            log.Fatalf("No nodes available to reply!")
    }
    log.Println("[Detected node]", inbox)

    payload := []byte("hi...")
    response, err := nc.Request(inbox, payload, 30*time.
    Second)
    if err != nil {
            log.Fatal(err)
    }

    log.Println("[Response]", string(response.Data))
}
```

Each requestor will make five attempts to find another node to which it can make a request. It may not seem as if we added a lot in terms of functionality compared to the example at the beginning, but we have made it possible to better audit, which is the layer that failed in handling the request. We also have faster signaling of when to scale out the number of subscribers—when the subscribers are so busy that they cannot even reply to their own inbox, rather than when the requests time out (see Listing 10-11).

Listing 10-11. Running Subscribers and Requestors

```
seq 10 | parallel -j 10 -u go run long-request-subscriber-4.go
...

seq 10 | parallel -j 10 -u go run very-long-request-3.go
...
2018/02/20 14:48:57 [Detected node] _
INBOX.10FZUCH1jL3d8wpGMlmHCd
2018/02/20 14:48:57 [Response] done!
2018/02/20 14:48:57 Retrying...
2018/02/20 14:48:57 [Inbox Request]
2018/02/20 14:48:57 [Detected node] _INBOX.
oWatb6T2Sbtxs9ACeLMDkc
2018/02/20 14:49:17 [Response] done!
2018/02/20 14:49:17 [Response] done!
2018/02/20 14:49:17 [Response] done!
```

Subscriptions with Heartbeats

In the previous examples, a request is being made and taking up to 30 seconds to wait for a response. Waiting 30 seconds for the result of an action might be too long sometimes, especially when there has been a processing error in the interim. Now that we know how to make unique subscriptions by using nats.NewInbox, we could leverage the API and enhance the way requests are handled in order to provide a sort of status for action that is being processed.

Listing 10-12 shows a Request/Response-based protocol using JSON as the encoding format. The requestor sends a request but also announces a subscription where it can receive heartbeats pertaining to events related to the request.

Listing 10-12. Subscription for Heartbeats

```
package main

import (
        "context"
        "encoding/json"
        "log"
        "time"

        "github.com/nats-io/go-nats"
)

type RequestWithKeepAlive struct {
        HeartbeatsInbox string `json:"hb_inbox"`
        Data            []byte `json:"data"`
}

func main() {
        nc, err := nats.Connect(nats.DefaultURL)
        if err != nil {
                log.Fatal(err)
        }

        hbInbox := nats.NewInbox()
        req := &RequestWithKeepAlive{
                HeartbeatsInbox: hbInbox,
```

```
            Data:                 []byte("hello world"),
    }
    payload, err := json.Marshal(req)
    if err != nil {
            log.Fatal(err)
    }

    ctx, cancel := context.WithTimeout(context.
    Background(), 30*time.Second)
    defer cancel()
    response, err := nc.RequestWithContext(ctx, "long.
    request", payload)
    if err != nil {
            log.Fatal(err)
    }

    log.Println("[Response]", string(response.Data))
}
```

Note that in order to have more control over the cancellation logic of the request, we are using the context package in Go.

Now let's set up the subscriber as Listing 10-13 shows. The subscriber expects to receive a JSON payload that it can decode, which includes the heartbeats inbox made by the requestor to receive status messages related to the request.

Listing 10-13. Scaffolding the Heartbeat Subscription

```
package main

import (
        "encoding/json"
        "log"
        "time"
```

```go
        "github.com/nats-io/go-nats"
)

type RequestWithKeepAlive struct {
        HeartbeatsInbox string `json:"hb_inbox"`
        Data            []byte `json:"data"`
}

func main() {
        nc, err := nats.Connect(nats.DefaultURL)
        if err != nil {
                log.Fatal(err)
        }
        nc.Subscribe("long.request", func(m *nats.Msg) {
                log.Println("[Processing]", string(m.Data))
                var req RequestWithKeepAlive
                err := json.Unmarshal(m.Data, &req)
                if err != nil {
                        log.Printf("Error: %s", err)
                        nc.Publish(m.Reply, []byte("error!"))
                        return
                }
                log.Printf("[Heartbeats] %+v", req)

                // Do the work
                time.Sleep(30 * time.Second)
                nc.Publish(m.Reply, []byte("done!"))
        })

        log.Println("[Started]")
        select {}
}
```

With that set up, let's go back to the requestor and implement the cancellation logic (see Listing 10-14). The requestor will be expecting to receive a few health-related events during the processing of the request at most every 10 seconds. Every time there is a heartbeat message emitted to the requestor, it will reset the deadline and let the processing continue. At the same time, the request is capped to take at most 30 seconds, as governed by the `context.WithTimeout` call.

Listing 10-14. Context Cancellation of via Timer

```go
package main

import (
        "context"
        "encoding/json"
        "log"
        "time"

        "github.com/nats-io/go-nats"
)
type RequestWithKeepAlive struct {
        HeartbeatsInbox string `json:"hb_inbox"`
        Data            []byte `json:"data"`
}

func main() {
        nc, err := nats.Connect(nats.DefaultURL)
        if err != nil {
                log.Fatal(err)
        }

        hbInbox := nats.NewInbox()
        req := &RequestWithKeepAlive{
                HeartbeatsInbox: hbInbox,
```

```go
        Data:                   []byte("hello world"),
    }
    payload, err := json.Marshal(req)
    if err != nil {
            log.Fatal(err)
    }

    ctx, cancel := context.WithTimeout(context.
    Background(), 30*time.Second)
    defer cancel()
    t := time.AfterFunc(10*time.Second, func() {
            cancel()
    })
    nc.Subscribe(hbInbox, func(m *nats.Msg) {
            log.Println("[Heartbeat] extending
            deadline...")
            t.Reset(10 * time.Second)
    })

    log.Println("[Request]")
    response, err := nc.RequestWithContext(ctx, "long.
    request", payload)
    if err != nil {
            log.Fatal(err)
    }

    log.Println("[Response]", string(response.Data))
}
```

Then the subscriber needs to implement a go routine that will be responsible for emitting the health events in order to prevent the requestor from giving up too soon (se Listing 10-15).

Listing 10-15. Active Subscription

```go
package main

import (
        "encoding/json"
        "log"
        "time"

        "github.com/nats-io/go-nats"
)

type RequestWithKeepAlive struct {
        HeartbeatsInbox string `json:"hb_inbox"`
        Data            []byte `json:"data"`
}

func main() {
        nc, err := nats.Connect(nats.DefaultURL)
        if err != nil {
                log.Fatal(err)
        }
        nc.Subscribe("long.request", func(m *nats.Msg) {
                log.Println("[Processing]", string(m.Data))
                var req RequestWithKeepAlive
                err := json.Unmarshal(m.Data, &req)
                if err != nil {
                        log.Printf("Error: %s", err)
                        nc.Publish(m.Reply, []byte("error!"))
                        return
                }
                log.Printf("[Heartbeats] %+v", req)

                t := time.NewTicker(5 * time.Second)
```

```
    defer t.Stop()
    go func() {
            for range t.C {
                    log.Println("[Heartbeat]")
                    nc.Publish(req.HeartbeatsInbox,
                    []byte("OK"))
            }
    }()

    // Long processing time...
    time.Sleep(20 * time.Second)
    nc.Publish(m.Reply, []byte("done!"))
})

log.Println("[Started]")
select {}
}
```

If the subscriber fails during the processing of the message, it will take
the requestor at most 10 seconds to consider the request as failed.

Gathering Multiple Responses

Sometimes we may want to receive more than one reply from a single
request; for example, if we want to determine how many subscribers are
out there. We may be able to devise a simple solution by using the NextMsg
API from a single subscription along with the context package in Go to
control the cancellation of the request.

In Listing 10-16, we have an N number of subscribers that will reply
with their own inboxes.

Listing 10-16. Simple Subscriber That Also Replies with an Inbox

```
package main

import (
        "log"

        "github.com/nats-io/go-nats"
)

func main() {
        nc, err := nats.Connect(nats.DefaultURL)
        if err != nil {
                log.Fatal(err)
        }
        log.Println("[Started]")

        inbox := nats.NewInbox()
        nc.Subscribe(inbox, func(m *nats.Msg) {
                log.Printf("Received message on inbox: %+v", m)
        })

        nc.Subscribe("collect", func(m *nats.Msg) {
                nc.Publish(m.Reply, []byte(inbox))
        })

        select {}
}
```

Similar to the heartbeat example, Listing 10-17 shows how we can use a timer to fire if it has passed too long since we have received a reply from a component. We expect all the healthy components in the system to reply as fast as possible. Note that there are two possible cancellation events that may occur—one is a five-second deadline set via context.WithTimeout and the other is the timer that will be extended two seconds each time it

254

gets a successful response. This way, if multiple requests continue arriving and extending the timer constantly, the gathering of responses will still be limited by the five-second deadline.

Listing 10-17. Gathering Multiple Replies

```
package main

import (
        "context"
        "log"
        "time"

        "github.com/nats-io/go-nats"
)

func main() {
        nc, err := nats.Connect(nats.DefaultURL)
        if err != nil {
                log.Fatal(err)
        }

        ctx, cancel := context.WithTimeout(context.
        Background(), 5*time.Second)
        defer cancel()
        t := time.AfterFunc(2*time.Second, func() {
                cancel()
        })

        inbox := nats.NewInbox()
        replies := make([]interface{}, 0)
        sub, err := nc.SubscribeSync(inbox)
        if err != nil {
                log.Fatal(err)
        }
```

```
        startTime := time.Now()
        nc.PublishRequest("collect", inbox, []byte(""))
        for {
                msg, err := sub.NextMsgWithContext(ctx)
                if err != nil {
                        break
                }
                replies = append(replies, msg)

                // Extend deadline on each successful response.
                t.Reset(2 * time.Second)
        }
        log.Printf("Received %d responses in %s", len(replies),
        time.Since(startTime))
}
```

There are some caveats to this approach, as there may be outliers that are too slow to reply within this time. In that case, we want to discard them intentionally, and instead leverage the fact that we got the replies of those that were the most healthy to work reliably in the system.

Summary

In this chapter, we saw a few of the advanced styles for using NATS to communicate. As we have seen, even though the APIs are fairly simple, they do enable for very sophisticated usage. It is possible to build on top of them certain Request/Response protocols that could fit even more use cases.

Index

A

Asynchronous I/O, 67–72

Authorization credentials, 50–51

B

Binary protocol, 20

C, D, E, F, G

Cloud Native Computing
　　Foundation (CNCF), 18

Cluster network topology, NATS

　　autodiscovery and load
　　　　balancers, 126–129

　　bootstrapping, 123–124

　　configuration, 114, 116–119

　　explicitly setting, 121–123

　　full-mesh topology, 113

　　monitoring port, 124–125

　　nodes, 113

　　server failure, 112

　　setting up clustering, 119, 121

　　three nodes, 111

H

Heartbeat subscription

　　active subscription, 252–253

　　context cancellation, timer,
　　　　250–251

　　scaffolding, 248–249

I, J, K

Inbox subscriptions

　　backing off, subscriber
　　　　busy, 240, 242

　　long request, 234–235

　　nats.NewInbox
　　　　API, 237

　　QueueSubscribe, load
　　　　balancing, 242–243

　　requestor timing
　　　　out, 236

　　requests, 238–239

　　retries, 244–245

　　running multiple subscribers in
　　　　parallel, 240

　　slow replies, 235–236

© Waldemar Quevedo 2018

W. Quevedo, *Practical NATS*, https://doi.org/10.1007/978-1-4842-3570-6

Inbox subscriptions (*cont.*)
    subscribers and requestors,
        running, 246
    unique subscription, 237–238

L

Lowest latency response, 40–41

M

Monitoring NATS
    server instrumentation
        client subscriptions, 180–182
        /connz endpoint, 175–176,
          178–180
        HTTP server, 169
        monitoring port, 169
        nats-top usage, 193–196
        /routez endpoint, 187–189,
         191, 192
        sorting and limiting
         query, 182–187
        /subsz endpoint, 192–193
        /varz endpoint, 170, 172–174
Multiple responses,
    gathering, 253–256

N, O

NATS
    authorization deadline, 100–101
    clustering options, 91
    clustering port, 91

and Configuration Opts, 93
configuring authorization, 98–100
customizing port and bind, 89–90
delivery guarantees, 10–11
demo.nats.io endpoint, 2
docker, 108–109
factor of, 4
full-mesh topology, 9
GitHub, 1
gnatsd, 88
Go NATS client, 16
Go programming language, 14
HTTP-based REST APIs, 4
HTTP endpoint, 89
interfaces, 92
Keepalive Interval, 104
load balancing, 7
logging outputs, 97–98
maximum number of
    connections, 104
maximum payload size, 102–103
message broker/queue, 11
microservices and cloud-native
    applications, 16–18
modern cloud architectures, 1
net/http package, 5
profiling port, 92–93
publish/subscribe messaging, 2
request/response flow, 6
roots, 12–14
server configuration, 85, 87
server logging, 94–96
server reloading

debug and trace logging
  levels, 105–106
max connections, 107–108
slow consumer error, 9
slow consumers handling, 103
Stale connection, 10
three-node cluster, 88
TLS Configuration Options, 101
NATS client
asynchronous I/O, 67–70, 72
authorization credentials, 50–51
client reconnection, 77–80
Close API, 82, 84
connect uses, 45–46
customization, 47
event callbacks, 80, 82
features, 43–44
Flush API, 62–63
Publish API, 51–52, 54
QueueSubscribe API, 57–58
reconnect buffer, 75–77
removing, subscription, 58–59,
  61–62
Request API, 63, 65
Request/Response
  protocol, 65, 67
state transitions, 73–74
Subscribe API, 51, 54–57
NATS protocol, 20
NATS Rider application
API Server, 134–136, 154
architecture, 133
base component, 137–139

component kit package, API
  Server, 145, 147–148
components, 132, 145
discovery and status
  subscriptions, 141
Driver Agent, 161–164, 166
event handlers
  implementation, 140
flow of request, 132
folder structure, 133–134
HandleRides function, 151, 153
HTTP Endpoints, 148–149
load balanced rider
  manager, 154–160
microservices architecture, 131
Request/Response
  types, 150–151
Rides Managers,
  QueueSubscribe, 150
SetupConnectionToNATS
  implementation, 139–140
SetupConnectionToNATS
  reusable logic, 142
status subscription, 143–144

P

PING/PONG protocol, 24
Protocol commands
  connecting to NATS, 22–23
  NATS Server, 21
  PING and PONG, 24
  PUB and SUB

Protocol commands (*cont.*)
    publish messages, 26
    queue subscriptions, load
      balancing, 34–36
    registering interest, 28
    request/response, 39–40
  UNSUB
    lowest latency response, 40–41
    removing interest,
      subscription, 37–38
    subscription identifier
      (sid), 36
  wildcards, 31–33

Q

Queue subscription, 34

R

Request/Response-based
    protocol, 247–248

S

Security, NATS
  authorization timeout, 201
  certificate authority, 201
  cfssl installation, 203
  crypto/tls package, 197
  custom root CA, 205
  EventMachine
    implementation, 197
  fields, 198
  monitoring endpoint, 200, 208
  required clients, 202

routes connections, 209–211
secure connection, 199
secure NATS infrastructure, 202
securing client
  connections, 206–207
security roles, 203–204
server setup, 198
Slow consumer protocol error
routes, 228–230
subscriptions, 226, 228
troubleshooting
  disconnection events, 225
  error callback, 225
  fast producer on bar, 221
  fast producer on foo, 220
  running publisher, 222–223
  setting up event
    handlers, 223–224
  tight loop, 222
  types of clients, 220
types of, 217, 219

T, U, V

TLS
  auto discovery and
    routes, 213–216
  command-line
    options, 212–213
  configuration blocks, 200
  openssl client, 212

W, X. Y, Z

Wildcards, 31–33

Printed in the United States
By Bookmasters